What If . . .
is dedicated to the power within us,
whether we see it or not,
whether we know it or not
or whether we choose to use it or not.

ACKNOWLEDGMENT

I wish to thank my husband, Clinton D. Chevalier
for support and encouragement,
for a faith that never wavers,
for a belief in me that never quits,
for days of asking "How far are you in the
book now?"
and for pushing when the spirits said so.
I see you "walking your talk."

INTRODUCTION

What If . . . is a book of daily readings for you, especially if you are a worrier like me. Maybe when you worry you ask yourself "What if . . . ?" too much. I have spent a lot of wasted time worrying. I now see worry as a choice I made for years. And now I have the power to change.

What If . . . is really the beginning note in my *Worry Song*. My thoughts begin with this note and gradually encompass the worst of outcomes. I rarely catch myself when I begin this chant. The only way I have found to stop *The Worry Song* is to stop myself in midnote and realize that my thoughts are not the only possible outcome of what can happen to me.

Over the years, I have also learned that there are solutions to almost all the problems I face, and I can learn to cope with those that have no solution. I have learned that a powerful resource lives within all of us. It is an incredible Force.

I am often surprised by the solutions my inner power reveals if given the chance to be heard. This assures me that we are all related to a Power greater than ourselves.

I am stubborn in giving up *The Worry Song* and the *What If . . . ?* chorus. I have given a lot of time to them over the years. I have sung their tune with great devotion. I have been loyal to self-doubt. I now wonder what I could have done with all the wasted time I spent worrying.

As a result of writing this book and "What If . . . ?" over 365 times, I can say I am tired of the phrase. That may be a good thing, since I still find myself singing it on occasion.

I hope you will do what I found myself doing, as you read this book, by turning "What

If . . ." inside out and finding a better and more positive empowering view. I could no longer be a slave to the "Master Worry." I found a way out.

As I turned "What If . . ." inside out, I found many curious gifts: the urge to take responsibility for how I think and act, the permission to feel whatever I feel, and the desire to take good care of myself. Beyond these gifts, there was always another way to see a previously worrisome situation.

I wish you courage as you read, the will to give up worry and turn it inside out, and the gift of *power* that is truly *you*.

A. J. Chevalier, Ph.D.
Buffalo, Wyoming

THE WORRY SONG

it seems to me that worry
is a way to fill my time
replacing all my inner strength
no reason or no rhyme

when my living could go well
i shoot that all to hell
i ask myself to worry
and weave a tale to tell

the trouble with this is
i believe the tale of pain
from there i find no comfort
just more worry and no gain

THE WORRY SONG ❦

i have to ask myself
just what is there to gain
by filling up the time i have
with systematic pain?

if there is a moment — one to spare
i do not let it go
i pack it in with "what if" din
a noisy chaos show.

all this goes on in my head
others do not see or hear it
they would talk me out of it
or they would come to fear it

worry and the "what if" thoughts
are scary things you know
contagious as the common cold
they will not let you go

so what's it matter if i do
my hours of life this way
no need to wonder what's gone under
or what slipped by me today

if I remembered once to ask
what could i build or think or say
i might give up "what if" thoughts
and find another way

it's just possible that all that din
that noise within my head
keeps me free from being me
and locks me up instead.

and so in never knowing me,
i can then safely say
i did not find what's truly mine
that takes some other day.

why i'm here, what i'm to do
is locked inside you see
guarded by the "what if" thoughts
so i can never be

all i'm called to be and do
all i'm called to learn and share
are packed in rubble and bring trouble
i'm left with just despair

and maybe if there's still a way
to find sound strength inside
i'd overcome the "what if" hum
and restore my health and pride.

A. J. Chevalier, Ph.D.
April 1994

WHAT IF...

I lose my way?
I am late to work?
I can't find a job?
I can't make new friends?
my children go to jail?
I lose my pocketbook?
I don't have enough money for groceries?
I can't pay the rent?
I lose in the stock market?
I can't finish school?
I can't do the work in school?
I can't finish my paper?
the phone company won't transfer our phone
     by Friday?
my friends think I am crazy?

I can't find a mate?
I lose everything I have worked for all these
    years?
I go bankrupt?
I am misunderstood?
s/he gets mad at me?
I get hurt?
I can never find anyone to live with me again?
I can't stop seeing him/her?
I can't focus on my work?
I am never well-known?
no one likes my work?
my parents disapprove of what I am doing?
I hate my job?
I can never find the right career/job for me?
I can't please my teachers?
I have to leave my area?
I have to train for another job?
he/she finds another woman/man?
my landlord won't give the deposit back?
I make a mistake on the report?
no one understands me?
I am early and no one is there?

❀

I get an ulcer from worrying?
I have to take care of my parents in their old
    age?
I can never have children?
I lose my children to a car accident?
I don't catch on quickly enough?
we have to add more paperwork at the office?
I am never hired again for another job?
no one sees my talents?
my partner dies?
I lose my house?
my car is broken into?
someone tries to rape me?
I have to do something over again?
I have no free time?
my children don't listen to me?
I lose the money my parents gave me?
it rains at the wrong time?
there is an accident?
I can't find anyone to help me?
I can't speak the language?
I trust too much and then pay for it later?
no one believes me?

I am left alone to defend myself?
I can't drive in the snow?
I have to give up my children?
I have to give up my pet?
I have to move into a nursing home?
no one comes to pick me up?
I run out of food?
I can't move everything I have?
I fall in love too fast?
I fall in love with the wrong person?
my family does not approve of my partner?
my family blames me for the family problems?
I can't figure out what my needs are?
I don't want to answer as soon as they want
    me to answer?
all the good men/women are taken?
there is no room for me in their plans?
my parents cut me off?
I need to tell my parents off and I'm too afraid
    to do it?
I get audited?
I don't make enough money?
I don't believe in myself enough?

❈

I find too many faults in myself?
I can't ever have my own home?
they pass me over for promotion?
they make fun of my ideas?
they laugh at me?
they tell me to do the job over again?
I have to take a job that is way below my skills
    and training?
I have to answer for someone else's behavior?
someone steals my idea?
there are no supplies left when I get there?
I can't make the car payments?
no one will speak up about the problem?
everyone expects me to explain the situation?
everyone leaves me all the work to do?
the kids don't do their chores?
my child quits speaking to me?
my children blame me for all their problems?
the teachers hate women/men?
there's a lot of prejudice at my job?
God doesn't answer my prayers the way I ask?
I am not sure what to do?
I am listening and I still don't understand?

they refuse to listen?
I make a request and they do not honor it?
I get fired?
I need work and can't get it?
I am too scared to move?
I have to wait a long time for an answer?
the people I believe in make big mistakes?
there is no one to listen to me when I need to
       talk?
I have too many problems all at once?
I feel overwhelmed by all my problems?
they never give me an answer?
I lose all hope?
there are no alternatives?
the only choice makes me sick?
I lose faith in God?
I lose faith in my religion?
I lose my place in line?
I lose the tickets?
there is not enough help to complete the job?
I am charged with a crime?
I have to go to jail?
I have to face my parents before I die?

❀

I die a slow and painful death?
I die alone?
I am rushed into a decision?
I can't find anyone to agree with me?
I can't make a living the way I want to?
I am wrongly accused?
I find out my parents violated me?
my rights are violated?
everyone else gives up on me?
I can't protect my children from harm?
I am laid off from my job?
I have to move to find work?
I find another partner just like my first one?
my partner and I disagree on just about every-
    thing?
my children expect me to do everything for
    them?
I get too dependent on others' opinions?
I want to leave my relationship?
I can't get my partner to see my point of view?
I have to pay more taxes than I thought?
I can't pay my bills?
I have to retire early?

I look different as I get older?

I gain too much weight?

I lose my beauty as I age?

I am mugged?

there's no way out of my situation?

I can't afford the services I need?

I can't stop thinking about my problem?

I can't stop talking about my problem?

there's a good chance I will "lose face" in front of others?

I stand alone on a particular issue?

I lose my dreams?

there are no opportunities open for me now?

I have to do something I hate to be able to pay the bills?

I have to work two jobs?

I want to work for myself and don't know how?

there is no need for my services?

no one lets me speak?

they don't understand that they need to pay for my services?

they put so much pressure on me that I can't stand it?

they put too much pressure on me?

I have an anxiety attack?

I forget some useful information?

I bring the wrong information?

no one likes my writing?

the people I respect the most don't like what
    I do?

other people don't keep their promises?

the person I trust most violates that trust?

my best friend makes a pass at my husband/
    wife?

my children lose faith in me?

the car won't start?

my project fails?

others blame me for their parts in a problem
    situation?

I take on others' problems, not knowing that I
    did this?

my children pick bad partners?

I don't know how to express how I feel?

I don't know what to do when I am sad?

I don't know what to do when I am angry?

I am lost in very heavy traffic?

I don't know what makes me really happy?

I don't know how to ask for what I want?

I don't fit in with anyone I know?

I feel left out?

I don't know how to start a conversation with others?

my partner has a problem that s/he doesn't know about?

my partner has a problem s/he can't solve?

I lose my license?

a friend's behavior threatens what I want to do?

my partner's behavior threatens what I want to do?

my partner's behavior threatens the safety of my children?

my spouse/ex-spouse hates our child?

I have writer's block?

no one understands what is most important to me?

I run out of time?

my children don't think I love them enough?

I am too scared to try?

I am in too much pain to think clearly?

they expect too much from me?

I expect too much from myself?

I can't learn the skills I need to keep my job?

my parents do not approve of the work I want
to do?

I lose my self-respect?

I no longer want to live?

there is no reason to live?

I am so scared that I want to run?

it seems like everyone is picking on me?

I make a promise I can't keep?

I agree to an unreasonable request and then
later change my mind?

I feel trapped by my partner?

I lose a part of my body to disease?

I find I don't want to cooperate with others
around me?

they keep adding more and more responsibilities on me without my consent?

they think I'm lazy?

they don't understand what I'm doing?

I don't understand what is happening to me?

I lose my faith?

I fail?

I fail a lot?

there's not enough of what I need?

I give up in the middle of an important project?

I lose my best friends?

I lose everything that means anything to me?

I have to answer for what I did?

I can't explain it well enough?

others think what I'm doing is a waste of my time and ability?

there's no time left for what I need?

I forget to ask myself what I need in any situation?

everyone around me thinks what I'm doing is crazy?

there's a lot to do and everyone thinks I ought to be doing it?

no one will share the load?

there aren't enough resources to go around?

I disappoint those close to me?

what is important to me changes?

I change what I think of myself?

I start taking care of myself first and put others second?

others say I am selfish?

others are better at this than I am?

others get along better with each other than they do with me?

someone tries to take my wife/husband?

my wife/husband has an affair?

I cannot support myself?

I am left all alone?

others keep interrupting my day and taking my time?

others want me to answer for my actions and I don't want to?

trying looks too hard?

I think my life is over?

I think I have a fatal disease?

I am afraid to go to the doctor?

my loved one is afraid to go to the doctor?

I lose the ability to think and reason?

I have to confront others with what they are doing to me?

they don't listen?

they tell me that I'm stupid?

they act like my opinions don't count?

they tell me to change my mind about what is important to me?

they make light of what is important to me?

they change the subject while I am telling them something that is very important to me?

they can't keep my secrets?

they discuss me when I am not around?

I can't see my way out of a tough situation?

I work too much ?

I have a hard time having fun?

the joy goes out of my life?

there is no one to talk to?

everyone gets the wrong idea about me?

everyone envies me?

my friends want what I have?

others do better than me?

I am not a good enough parent?

I get caught in traffic?

no one sees how hard I am trying?

my last resort fails?

I feel trapped in my relationship?

I'd rather be doing something else?

I'd rather be someone else?

no one ever knows I was here?

I'd rather be somewhere else?

people tear down my work?

others want me to fail?

others want me to do their hard work for them?

they are good at getting me to believe I should do their work?

I can't figure out what my part of a problem is from someone else's?

I have to be away from my wife/husband for too long?

work takes too much time away from my family?

I feel all alone?

I feel weak?

I feel strong?

people question my motives?

I fear losing the happiness I've found?

I can't get the information I need to solve my
    problem?
I can't find medical care for my child?
I can't afford medical care for my family?
someone breaks into my house?
someone turns me down again and again?
there is no way to get what I want?
I am a successful person and don't know what
    to do with it?
I can't get everything done in one day?
I have to wait longer than I had planned to
    reach my goal?
I change my goal in the middle of trying
    in order to reach another?
I had a good day?
I met someone and fell in love?
I could not stop worrying?
someone I fear challenged me to talk about it?
I had fewer friends?
my friends were all displeased with me at the
    same time?
I put family responsibilities first?
I put my own needs before the needs of others?

XXX

I stood up for what I believe in?

I felt stretched between important demands on my time?

I met the love of my life?

I was successful in business?

I took less time for others and spent more time on my own interests?

my friends reacted strangely to some of my choices?

my friends stopped being my friends because of my choices?

my work was honored by many?

I took care of my inner child?

there were fewer moments in the day when I fretted over what to do?

I required others to pay me what I am worth?

I made a good investment and it took time to pay it off?

I made a bad investment?

I made solid agreements with customers?

I stuck to my requirements for what is important to me?

I let others know how I feel when I feel it?

I held on to the way I feel?

I made a point to check in with myself about
how I feel?

there is not enough time, money or love?

I spent too much time worrying about others'
feelings?

I think that I'm the cause of others' feelings?

I lost what I know and learned a new way?

my life were simpler?

I gave up the idea of "mistakes"?

I saw all the events in my life as lessons?

there was a way to love myself more?

I really started loving myself?

I treated myself like I treated others I love?

I became really good at nurturing myself?

I had to live with very few things?

I lost all the weight I thought I should lose?

I kept fit and trim?

I put on more weight?

I had a dream and began it right now?

I saw my dream coming to life the way I want?

I knew that my dream would somehow help
others?

I was the only one who believed in my dream?

I could keep my sense of personal power?

I risked everything to live my dream?

others would not have risked everything for their dreams?

I used faith the size of a mustard seed?

I saw my mountains moving?

I chose to clear the air each time it needed to be done?

I moved the barriers between me and others?

I made decisions based on my needs?

I paid really close attention to what I want to do?

I honor all the feelings I have?

I have good friendships that work?

I have a good marriage and it works?

I feel joy and it no longer scares me?

I have a feeling and let it come and go?

the way was made clear for me to do what I want?

I cleared the way for me to be me?

I thought less of others' opinions and more of my own?

XXXIII

I had special work to do?
I saw myself as unique?
I began to be successful?
I left behind ways that no longer work for me?
I began to love my body?
I began to love my mind?
I began to love what is in my heart?
I accepted myself just as I am?
I said good things to myself all day long?
I presented myself in a positive light to others?
I examined my thoughts?
I examined my thoughts to see how they affect
   my feelings?
I paid no attention to those who criticize my
   attempt to be happy?
I gave myself a family of others who really
   support me?
I accept my family members for who they are?
I quit trying to change my family members?
I forgave my family?
I forgave others?
I forgave myself?
I lived life just the way I wanted to?

❀

I was praised for my work?

I had started life with all I needed?

I had what I needed when I was a child?

my parents had supported things I wanted to do?

I had all I needed now?

I let myself get angry when I was angry?

I let myself feel sorrow when I was sad?

I knew I did a good job?

I chose my principles over others' ideas of what I should be doing?

everyone thought I abandoned them?

I let go of expectations of others?

resentment became a thing of my past?

I helped myself and others in a balanced way?

I recognized my own talents?

I used my own talents?

I experienced joy in using my talents?

I developed my talents?

I believed all people make a contribution to the planet?

I became ready to work on my own hopes and dreams?

I offered myself to my Higher Power/God?

my life became an adventure?

I found that I could create my life as I wanted it to be daily?

I found that I could choose my reactions to things?

I chose meanings for things in my life and these gave me joy?

I found that I loved what I do?

my work became a joy for me?

I had nowhere to go?

I found all of life to be sacred?

I found myself to be sacred?

I found that others had the same feelings I do?

JANUARY

❧

*I am hungry
for my power*

WHAT IF...

I FIND THAT I AM STRONGER THAN I THINK I AM?

Then I can look at how my thoughts affect my strength. I can relax my ideas about my strength so that I can see just how strong I am.

—and—

I can move to do the things I need to do. If I choose the words that affect my strength, then I can make my strength what it needs to be at any time.

❀

I am as strong as the words I use to describe my strength.

❀

WHAT IF . . .

I CAN'T KEEP MY RESOLUTIONS ABOUT THE CHANGES I WANT TO MAKE?

Then I can look at the kinds of promises I make to myself. If I fail to keep them, I can determine realistic expectations of myself.

—and—

I can set reasonable limits on what I ask of myself. With these limits I can set reasonable goals with steps of success to achieve and celebrate.

❀

I make promises to myself that are reasonable. I learn from the ones I keep and the ones I throw out.

WHAT IF . . .

I SAID GOOD THINGS TO MYSELF
ALL DAY LONG?

First, what good things do I need to hear today? What will be different for me on this day? Can I turn this day around by what I say to myself all through the day?

—and—

I can learn to accept compliments from myself and others. I accept the good in me. I can change the course of my day by what I say to myself.

❀

I choose the course of my day by what I say to myself.

❀

WHAT IF . . .

MY LIFE WERE SIMPLER?

Then I would have to learn to live in a simple way. I would learn the very basic things that are vital to me. I would keep what is important and discard many things that only seemed important.

—and—

I would learn simple pleasures and easier ways. Most things that discourage me now would lose their hold on me. I would return to what is natural for me.

❀

Living simply helps me focus on what is really important to me.

❀

WHAT IF . . .

I THINK I AM THE CAUSE OF OTHERS' FEELINGS?

Then I will feel responsible for the lion's share of all relationships. I will only be at peace when all my relationships are running smoothly. I will get tired often.

—and—

If I am tired, I can learn to use this as a clue that I have done too much. Then I can set new limits for myself. I can accept responsibility only for the part of relationships that is mine. I will have more energy for the things that are important to me.

❀

I can recognize and take care of my part in relationships. I can let others do the same.

❀

WHAT IF . . .

I BEGAN TO LOVE MY BODY?

Then I would stop sending it hate messages. I would stop comparing myself to others. My health would improve and so would my sense of well-being. I would take responsibility for the way I look *and* the way I look at myself.

—and—

I alone would decide what is good for my body. I would naturally be drawn to what my body needs. What it does not need would fall away from me. I would practice the kind of self-care I really need.

❀

My body needs loving messages.

WHAT IF . . .

I CHALLENGED MY BOSS/MY TEACHER?

Then I would learn more about taking risks. I would show a strong side of me to others. Others would get the chance to understand what is important to me. I would be taking good care of what is important to me.

—and—

I would learn what it takes to get along with this person. I would learn what is important to him/her. We could reach a new understanding that would guide us to get along with each other in a new way.

❀

Taking risks allows me to learn the things I want to know.

WHAT IF . . .

MY FRIENDS REACT STRANGELY TO SOME OF MY CHOICES?

Then I have the opportunity to stand my ground and support what is important to me. I can choose to explain or not. This offers me the chance to set new boundaries for myself. This offers each of us the chance to know one another on a deeper level.

—and—

I can continue to choose the ways that are right for me. I can loosen myself from the need for the approval of others.

❀

Right action comes easily to me. My choices need only be approved by me.

9

WHAT IF . . .

I LEFT BEHIND WAYS THAT NO LONGER WORK FOR ME?

Then I would find new ways that fit me better. I would feel discomfort that goes along with changing. I would come to see this as a natural part of any change. I would have the chance to accept all the feelings that go with this change.

—and—

I would learn to deal with others' reactions to the change in me. I would see the influence I have on them by their reactions. Their reactions, good or bad, would give me clues to how I need to support my new ways.

❊

New ways mean change and change means discomfort. I can deal with discomfort by seeing it as natural.

❈

WHAT IF . . .

PEOPLE QUESTION MY MOTIVES?

Then I can learn how it feels to have my motives questioned. I can search deep within myself and learn more about my own reasons for doing what I am doing. I can figure out what I may need to correct.

—and—

I can correct whatever needs correcting. I can learn to let go of the need for approval from others or I can use their remarks to understand myself in a deeper way. I can choose to let their remarks fit me or not.

❈

When others question my motives, it deepens my understanding of myself.

WHAT IF . . .

SOMEONE TURNS ME DOWN AGAIN AND AGAIN?

Then I can look at the way I approach them. I can see if I need to change my approach. I can also learn that I don't fit with everyone and that this is normal. I can learn that rejection with one person does not mean rejection with all.

—and—

I can decide on new ways to approach others. I can decide if this is really my problem or someone else's problem. Either way, I learn from both.

❀

Being turned down gives me the chance to find a better fit for what is important to me.

❀

WHAT IF . . .

TRYING LOOKS TOO HARD?

Then I have the chance to reassess how I can approach my situation. If I have tried too long and too hard, then I may need to rest from my efforts.

—*and*—

I may learn to let go and refuse to try so hard. I can look at what is better for me when I do not try so hard. When I try less, others may do more.

❀

I can trust my eyes and ears to tell me when to stop trying.

❃

WHAT IF . . .

THEY DISCUSS ME WHEN
I AM NOT AROUND?

Then I am free from hearing anything that might upset me. I am free from dealing with issues that may be discussed by others. I only have responsibility for what I choose to be a part of and know about.

—and—

I can realize that others have the right to their own opinions. I do not have to know what others are saying about me. It is enough to deal with what they say to me.

❃

I choose whether I will be influenced by what others say about me.

❈

WHAT IF . . .

OTHERS KEEP INTERRUPTING MY DAY AND TAKING MY TIME?

Then my day will be full of their chaos and it will go according to their needs. My own needs will take a backseat to everything else.

—and—

I now have the chance to restructure my day to suit me. I also have the chance to help others know my needs. I can set the boundaries I need. Inside those boundaries I can better take care of my own needs.

❈

When others interrupt my process, it is a clue for me to check my boundaries.

❀

WHAT IF . . .

SOMEONE I FEAR CHALLENGES ME TO TALK ABOUT IT?

Then I have the chance to speak up on my own behalf and express my needs to this person. I have the chance to feel my fear and walk through it by responding to the challenge.

—and—

I have the chance to clear the air between us, take care of my own needs and work through the fear, all at the same time.

❀

When I challenge my fear of another person, I take care of my needs while clearing the air, and I transform my fear into something useful.

❀

WHAT IF . . .

I LEARNED SOMETHING I REALLY WANTED TO LEARN?

Then I would step into the world of my own dreams. I would find steps that are comfortable and some that are dangerously exciting. I would begin to make them real for myself. My dreams would become what I live every day.

—and—

I would come to know the joy in my own curiosity. I would be following my heart's desire. I would know a genuine sense of bliss that comes from making my own choices.

❀

Learning what I want to learn is attending to my natural state of curiosity.

WHAT IF . . .

I QUIT TRYING TO CHANGE MY FAMILY MEMBERS?

Then I might have a lot of time on my hands that I didn't have before. I might know a new peace of mind. By letting go of trying to change others, I free myself to find my own happiness.

—and—

Letting go of expectations of others allows me to pursue my own interests. I can let others find their own solutions. When I get out of the way, they will learn what they need to learn in their own best way.

❦

Letting others change in their own ways, frees me to change in my own way.

❃

WHAT IF . . .

I CHOSE JOYFUL MEANINGS FOR THE THINGS IN MY LIFE?

Then I would have to give up complaining about how awful things are. I would approach each event with playful curiosity and let myself learn what to do next. In each situation, learning would be fun.

—and—

My complaining would be replaced with my own efforts to learn more about myself. I would experience a new peace of mind. I would once again enjoy the curiosity I knew as a small child.

❃

The meanings I choose for the events in my life can spark my curiosity and help me to learn new things.

❀

WHAT IF . . .

I HAVE TO ANSWER FOR WHAT I DID?

Then I will know what it means to be responsible for my own actions. I will have the chance to think about what I did by examining my own actions. I will be able to see how my decision was made. I will be able to determine if I need to change.

—and—

Others will see a strong person in me as I stand behind what I did. They will see a person able to admit to wrongdoing or stand up for a principle. They will see, in me, a good example of responsible behavior.

❀

When I answer for what I do, I show responsibility and personal integrity.

❄

WHAT IF . . .

I HATE MY JOB?

Then feelings of frustration and unhappiness will overwhelm me from time to time. These feelings can help guide new action to improve the situation. Hating my job is a sign of the need for a better fit between the work I do and me.

—and—

This need for a better fit may push me to find a better job. I can take my feelings and use them as fuel to prepare for another job, to find another job and to change the work that I do.

❄

I refuse to be controlled by work that I hate to do.

❧

WHAT IF . . .

THEY THINK I AM LAZY?

Then I may feel criticized and overburdened with others' opinions of me. I may realize that there is some truth to what they are saying or that things only appear that way. I have the choice to change my behaviors.

—and—

Their opinion of me may never change. I now have the chance to decide whose opinion is most important to me. It is for me to determine what I do, how I do it and when.

❧

I can, when I need to, alter my opinion of myself and my actions.

❀

WHAT IF . . .

THEY MAKE LIGHT OF WHAT IS IMPORTANT TO ME?

Then I will instantly feel dishonored. I will feel uncomfortable, even scared to move on my own behalf. I may feel confused about how to respond.

—and—

I can realize that I am not locked into any particular response. I can take this moment to get really clear about what is important to me. I can once again choose to back up what I feel. I can confront others or choose to remove myself from any disrespectful situation.

❀

No matter what others do, I can do what honors me.

❀

WHAT IF . . .

I THINK I HAVE A FATAL DISEASE?

Then I may feel fear, anxiety and dread. This will affect everything I do, think and feel. My body, mind and spirit will be affected. I may feel controlled by my circumstances.

—*and*—

I can still choose how I will react. I can choose to verify what I think is the problem. I can choose to know the reality of my situation. I can choose the meaning I will attach to the outcome of knowing about my own health.

❀

*I can choose meaning for
any event in my life.*

WHAT IF . . .

I AM NOT A GOOD ENOUGH PARENT?

Then my children might suffer because of what I do with them. I might be too harsh or too lenient with them. I might be too harsh on myself for not knowing more. My children might pose really tough situations to get me to think more about what I can do.

—and—

Each tough situation can push me to think about all the ways I might work with my children. The tough situations will draw out my ability to solve problems, or they can offer me the chance to get help from others. I can determine what is working for me as a parent and where I may need help.

❀

To be the kind of parent I want to be, I will look at my own ways, see what needs my attention and ask for help when I need it.

WHAT IF . . .

I GAVE UP THE IDEA OF "MISTAKES"?

Then I would have to look at all the things I do in a new way. It is easy to calculate a mistake. It is much harder to grow from the lesson learned there. If I no longer believed in mistakes, I might have to give up being so hard on myself.

—and—

I would be more open to learn from all the situations in my life. No event could control me. My days would be full of lessons. Each event would offer a personalized classroom for my human growth.

❀

If mistakes are really lessons, my fear is changed to curiosity.

❈

WHAT IF . . .

I LOSE WHAT I KNOW AND HAVE TO LEARN A NEW WAY?

Then I will feel sad, and I may want to cover up or deny the loss. I will feel that something is missing, and that I cannot get it back. I may also be angry for having to give up things that worked for me in the past.

—and—

I can gradually accept that something I have not yet learned is needed to solve my dilemma. I have the chance to fully feel my loss and move to the next phase of adjustment. I may reach new ways by trial and error, which is perfectly natural. Then I can teach myself what to do next.

❈

If I lose what I know, I can replace it with a new way to help myself.

❀

WHAT IF . . .

I KEPT FIT AND TRIM?

Then would I fear others' reactions to me? Would I feel whole as a person in my body? I might ask if I did this for me or because I gave in to the pressure of others? Would I feel more comfortable in a lighter body?

—and—

Would I recognize the benefits to me if I kept fit and trim? Is this a healthy concern or a mindless gesture of compliance with society's focus on being "thin"? How do I feel in this body? Am I the main source of my approval?

❀

I know the size my body needs to be. When I am at home with the size of my body, I feel a deep peace.

❦

WHAT IF . . .

I FORGIVE MYSELF?

Then I may find this a very hard choice to make. I may feel that I couldn't help the choices that I made. Or I may feel that I am human and make errors. If I forgive myself, then I can ask, "What is new for me?" Do I get more chances to make better choices?"

—and—

I may free myself to try something again or in a new way. I can allow myself to experiment with ways of doing things. I can see myself as fully human. I can be part of the big family of humans who, from time to time, know they must forgive themselves.

❦

Forgiving myself frees me.

❀

WHAT IF . . .

I BECAME REALLY GOOD AT NURTURING MYSELF?

Then others might become annoyed with my new focus. They might get angry with me. They might assume that something is wrong with me and act hurt. They might even insist that I change back to the way I was. Or they might walk away.

—and—

Some of them might see my need to take time for myself and to care for myself. Some might see it as a good example to follow. If I nurture myself, I get the chance to see who really supports me with this and who is around only to use what I offer them.

❀

When I nurture myself, I attract those who will support me in this process. Surrounding myself with their support helps me nurture myself.

❀

WHAT IF . . .

I HAD A DREAM AND BEGAN TO MAKE IT COME TRUE NOW?

Then I might have to protect it from the envy of others who have not yet realized their dreams. I might feel alone as I give more attention to my dream. The more energy I give to my dream, the more I make it work. Others may suddenly feel left out when I work on my dream.

—and—

When I work on my dream, others may see it and tap the courage inside themselves to start on their own dreams. I will feel a new joy in accomplishment.

❀

I get an extreme sense of joy in beginning my dream.

WHAT IF . . .

I PRESENTED MYSELF IN A POSITIVE LIGHT TO OTHERS?

Then I might be faced with questions and suspicion about what I am doing. Others may actually feel very uncomfortable with how I present myself. I might feel their scrutiny. They may allow their insecurities to direct their behavior and try to drain my energy.

—and—

This gives me the opportunity to practice protecting the positive posture I have chosen for myself. Others might also decide this is changing me in a good way. They might be curious about how to see themselves in a similar way. The energy between us might feel like a needed boost.

❀

***I can present myself to others in a
positive light and protect this image
from negative response.***

FEBRUARY

I am hungry
for my power
not to control
but to remember

❀

WHAT IF . . .

I LEARNED TO FOCUS ON CHANGING MYSELF?

Then I would have to look at what needs changing in me. I would have to look at my behavior, and that might make me feel very uncomfortable. It may be easier to look outward to change others than to focus on changing myself.

—and—

I now have the chance to make real change. I find that I can really only change my own behavior. No amount of trying on my part has ever changed others. If I keep the focus on myself, I can make changes in any situation.

❀

Keeping the focus on myself means I can change any situation I face.

❀

WHAT IF . . .

I HAVE TO CONFRONT OTHERS WITH WHAT THEY ARE DOING TO ME?

Then I will have to examine exactly what is harmful to me and what I want others to do differently. I must think about what my needs are and put them into words.

—and—

This may be a first for me. Or it just may be new to me. I can breathe in deeply, tell myself I have the right to air my concerns and tell others what I need. They also have the same right. Hearing this from one another is the beginning of changing my situation for the better.

❀

I speak to others about what I need from them, and I listen to what they need from me.

WHAT IF . . .

THEY KEEP ADDING MORE AND MORE RESPONSIBILITIES ON ME WITHOUT MY APPROVAL?

Then I will have to decide what my limits are. This may be hard for me, especially if my habit is to take on too much. I may even have to decide if I have any limits and then, if I do, I'll have to decide what to do about them.

—and—

I now have the chance to say what those limits are and to set new boundaries on what others can expect from me. I also have the chance to spend my time, energy and other resources on what pleases me.

❀

I can determine my own limits in any situation and choose to speak up on my own behalf.

❋

WHAT IF . . .

I FORGIVE OTHERS?

Then I can look for a change in myself. I do not have to talk myself into forgiving others. I do not have to do what is uncomfortable for me. I can simply make the choice to forgive others and move on with what I need to do in my life.

—and—

Forgiving frees me from the ties that bind up my energy in expecting others to change to suit me. I give up the need for them to change, and I get back all the energy I had tied up in waiting for them to change. I can choose to make these people a part of my life or not.

❋

***Forgiving others frees me
and my energy.***

WHAT IF . . .

I LET MYSELF FEEL SAD
WHEN I AM SAD?

Then I may be uneasy with this feeling. I will not only feel sad, but I will want the sad feeling to go away. It is often hard to sit with an uncomfortable feeling.

—and—

If I choose to honor my sad feeling, and sit with it for a while, it will pass and become another feeling. Feelings come and go; not one of them stays forever. If I choose to feel the sadness and cry when I need to, I will eventually be able to let it go. The part of me that was sad will feel taken care of.

❀

I am taking care of myself when I let myself feel sadness when it comes.

❀

WHAT IF . . .

I LET GO OF MY EXPECTATIONS OF OTHERS?

Then I also let go of trying to control the outcome of every situation in my life. I will have to give up trying to control others as well. I will let go of resentment when things don't go my way. I will have a lot more energy to use elsewhere.

—and—

With a lot more energy I will be faced with some new choices. I will have to decide what to do with my energy, time and resources that went into controlling people, places, and things. I may be faced with setting new goals for myself.

❀

When I let go of my expectations of others, I have a lot more energy for my own needs.

❀

WHAT IF . . .

THEY TELL ME TO DO THE JOB OVER AGAIN?

Then I will have to learn about others' expectations of me. I will have to get really clear about what others want. This may mean I have to ask questions to get it right or listen more carefully.

—*and*—

I have the chance to show others that I care about the quality of what I produce. It also shows that I care about meeting their needs as well as my own. I also have the chance to learn more about the task I am doing.

❀

In doing something over, I can learn more and produce work that makes me proud.

40

❀

WHAT IF . . .

I FIND TOO MANY FAULTS
IN MYSELF?

Then I will surely be hard to live with. If I spend time beating myself up for all my bad points, then my view of everything will be grim. I will find nothing that I can do right. I will likely approach others in the same way.

—and—

I can choose to take stock of what needs work in me on a regular basis. I can work on changes. When I get tired of beating myself up, I can take this as a clue that I need to lighten up. I can then set reasonable expectations and refuse to judge my own efforts so harshly.

❀

I can let go of the need to beat up on myself and replace that with regular examination of what I need to change. I can honor any effort I make.

WHAT IF . . .

I CAN'T GET MY PARTNER TO SEE MY POINT OF VIEW?

Then I can look at how I am approaching him/her. I can decide if I need to change my approach. I can also decide how important my concerns are and whether they need immediate attention. I may be in the position of having to decide if my partner is who I need to be with.

—and—

I have the chance to look at what is really important to me, and I can begin to state this in ways that my partner can hear. I have the chance to examine if I want to set different limits with him/her. I can give up persuading to see if my partner will meet me halfway and respond to my concerns.

❁

I can look at what is important to me, say it in a good way and support my concerns.

❀

WHAT IF . . .

I RESPECTED THE DIFFERENCES BETWEEN MYSELF AND OTHERS?

Then I would have to give up the idea that I know the "Truth" for everyone. I would have to give up the idea that I know what is best for everyone. I would have to give up trying to convince others of my ideas.

—and—

I would have to open myself to new ideas, experiences and maybe some discomfort. I would have to suspend what I know for something I do not know. I would see others' paths as valid as my own.

❀

When I open myself to differences in others, I gain by learning about their ways.

43

WHAT IF . . .

I LOSE MY INHERITANCE?

Then I will have to deal with the feelings I have about loss and making up the difference on my own. Maybe I will have to look at "making it" on my own. I may face a struggle as I learn to provide for myself.

—and—

As I provide for myself, I will learn that I have ways to do this. I will learn about my talents and abilities to keep myself going. I will learn what it takes to keep going. And I will have a new sense of my own strength.

❀

Money problems give me the chance to find new ways available to support me.

❊

WHAT IF . . .

I MADE A GOOD INVESTMENT AND IT TOOK TIME TO PAY OFF?

Then I would need to keep one eye on the future and one eye on the present. I may feel uncomfortable now without any immediate return on my time, funds or work, but I can outline the steps I need to take to insure that my investment pays off.

—and—

I can begin these steps now. I can look at what I can do today to begin these steps. I can place my hope in my own hard work.

❊

I can take the necessary steps to secure a good investment.

45

WHAT IF . . .

I CAN'T GET THE SKILLS I NEED TO KEEP MY JOB?

Then I am faced with some decisions. Have I looked at all my possibilities for getting these skills? Is this a money or child care issue? Have I exhausted all the resources I have? Are there some people in my community who know how to get these skills? Do I want to keep my job?

—*and*—

I can ask myself if I really want these skills. Or am I afraid to try something new? Is my fear keeping me from learning? I can choose to see my fear as normal for anyone trying something new. I can list my questions and find someone to help me.

❀

I can make the right decisions about my job and the skills I need.

❀

WHAT IF . . .

THEY ARE GOOD AT GETTING ME TO BELIEVE I SHOULD DO THEIR WORK?

Then it may be time to think about how often I allow this to happen to me. I may need to think about how I let them convince me that their work is really mine. I may need to ask myself what I get out of this arrangement, and how I keep it going in this way.

—*and*—

I can look at the toll it takes on me. If it is a big toll, I can look at what I need to change to suit me. I can ask myself what would suit me better. I can list my own needs and decide how I want to make these known to others.

❀

When others try to get me to do their work, I can decide if it is really something I want to do.

47

WHAT IF . . .

I CAN'T FIGURE OUT WHAT
MY NEEDS ARE?

Then this is a clue that I need much more time
and practice in figuring this out. In each situation
where I find myself feeling uncomfortable, I can
stop and refuse to commit to anything further. I
can look inside myself for what is missing.

—and—

I can ask myself if my need is physical, emotional or spiritual. My answer to this question is
always the right answer. I can trust what comes
into my mind. I need only give myself the time
and ask myself the questions. There is no hurry.

❀

*I have all the time I need to figure out
what I require in any situation.*

❀

WHAT IF . . .

I HAVE TO TAKE A JOB THAT I FEEL IS BENEATH ME?

Then I have the chance to meet my needs in a way I have not tried before. I have the chance to deal with my own discomfort about work that I dislike. I can use the discomfort I feel to keep searching for a job that suits me better.

—and—

I can make new choices that get me to a place where I want to be or help me cope with where I am. I can learn to use patience as I search for what I want to be and tolerance for where I am.

❀

Taking a job that is beneath me offers me the chance to develop patience and tolerance. I can grow from the discomfort I feel.

WHAT IF . . .

I THOUGHT LESS OF OTHERS' OPINIONS AND MORE OF MY OWN?

Then I would give up comparing myself to others and using them as an example for how I live. I may feel that I'm lacking personal goals.

—and—

I would become responsible for setting an example for myself and figuring out what pleases me. I would set my own goals and work to achieve them.

❀

By putting my opinions of myself first, I am free to set my goals according to what pleases me.

❀

WHAT IF . . .

I LEFT BEHIND EVERYONE'S DEFINITION OF WHO I AM AND DEFINED MYSELF?

Then I would be faced with their emotional reactions to the changes in me. I would have to resist responding to them in the same old ways. I would have to define myself in the new way, while dealing with their responses that say "change back."

—and—

As they tell me to change back, I will have to make decisions that will help support the new way I look at myself, even though it is hard work. I can list all the possible responses that will support the new me. I can choose ways that support the new me.

❀

It is natural for others to want me to respond to them in the way they know me. When I change, I can also choose ways to respond that will support the new me.

51

❀

WHAT IF . . .

I FOUND THAT I COULD CHOOSE MY REACTIONS TO WHATEVER HAPPENS TO ME?

Then I would no longer feel locked into one way of responding. I would not suffer from rash decisions. I could take my time and think about how I want to respond and what response helps me most.

—and—

I could figure out the best response for me in any situation. I could choose what any event means to me. I could choose a meaning that I could live with—one that supports the view I have of myself.

❀

If I choose the meanings of my situations, I can then choose a response that helps me.

WHAT IF . . .

I FOUND A BALANCE BETWEEN HELPING MYSELF AND HELPING OTHERS?

Then I might have to disappoint others who have received a lot of help from me. I might have to spend more time on figuring out my own needs. I would be faced with more decisions about whose needs came first.

—and—

I would have the chance to practice taking good care of myself. I would have the chance for better physical and emotional health. I would improve my ability to deal with others' disappointments and help them learn what I need. My relationships could improve if others knew my true needs.

❊

I need a balance between helping myself and helping others; this would help my health and improve my relationships.

❧

WHAT IF . . .

I BECAME MORE ASSERTIVE?

Then I would be asking others to deal with a change in me. They might be surprised or shocked, and I would have to deal with their reactions. Some would try asking me to change back to my old way. I would have to decide if I liked myself with the new way or the old way.

—and—

I can take all the time I need to decide how I want to respond or if I want to respond. I will also have to decide how to respond to each situation in the new way. To do this, I must accept my own needs in each new situation that I face, and I must want to take care of them. I must choose to voice my own needs.

❧

***Being assertive means knowing my
needs, wanting to take care of them
and letting others know that I will.***

❋

WHAT IF . . .

I KNEW THAT MY DREAM WOULD SOMEHOW HELP OTHERS?

Then I would have to decide how important it is to me to help others. I would have to decide what role helping others has in my life.

—and—

I may feel overwhelmed with the possibilities of what my dream can accomplish for others. I may feel that everything has to be done today or right away. I may find that I lose myself in the doing. I would have to find a balance between meeting my own needs and helping others.

❋

I can find the right balance between my own needs and the needs of others as I reach for my dream.

❖

WHAT IF . . .

I FEEL THAT I CAN'T COOPERATE WITH OTHERS AROUND ME?

Then I would need to determine what is not working well in my situation, and what I need to do about it. I may find that situations and people change in ways that no longer fit me as well as they once did. I can name what is missing for me.

—and—

I can determine if I can get what I need in my current situation. I can list other ways to meet my needs. I can also take this chance to see what it would take from me to cooperate with others around me. I can ask myself if this is something I want to do.

❖

When I cannot cooperate with others, I need to go inside myself and ask what I need. I can then move on to take care of my own needs.

❃

WHAT IF . . .

I FEEL STRETCHED BETWEEN THE DEMANDS PLACED ON ME?

Then I need to look at realistic limits for myself. I can place all the demands I feel in order of importance. Then I can release myself from the ones I do not choose. I have this right. I can also look at what I am doing that keeps a high number of demands on me.

—and—

I can look at what demands are realistic for me. I do not have to be perfect or even good at figuring this out. I only need to try to set realistic expectations for myself and learn about future choices from those I make today.

❃

When there are too many demands on me, I have the right to change them and the ability to figure out how to make it easier on myself.

57

❦

WHAT IF . . .

I DIDN'T PAY ANY ATTENTION TO THOSE WHO CRITICIZE MY ATTEMPT TO BE HAPPY?

Then I might lose the attention I'm used to getting from some people. I might lose some people I feel are my friends. I might find it necessary to confront others and let them see my feelings.

—and—

I might have to go inside myself and reexamine what I am doing that makes me happy. I would have to decide whose problem is upsetting my happiness. I may have to conclude that there is nothing I can do to change the opinions of others. I may have to let go of trying to convince them.

❦

In dealing with others' criticism, I decide whose opinion I will value most. If I value my own opinion, I am free to make choices that support my happiness.

❊

WHAT IF . . .

THEY PUT SO MUCH PRESSURE ON ME THAT I CAN'T STAND IT?

Then I will have to look within for the courage to address my own needs. I will have to find the willingness to make a decision on my own behalf. I can choose to confront them or I can remove myself from my situation.

—and—

I may have to find my own limits of what I am able or willing to tolerate. Once I know my limits, I can decide on ways to protect them. I can choose a way that will help me.

❊

Even under extreme pressure, I can look within myself for my limits and find a way to protect them.

✤

WHAT IF . . .

I AGREE TO A REQUEST AND THEN LATER FIND THE REQUEST UNREASONABLE?

Then I have the right to change my mind. I will have to deal with others' disappointment when I don't follow through. I can search my feelings to realize why the request bothers me and state it to the person in simple terms, such as: "This is unfair to me because . . ."

—and—

I can refuse to do something I once agreed to do if it no longer serves my interest. I only need my own permission to change my mind. I can remind myself of the consequences of this decision and list ways to handle the results of my choices.

✤

I can decide at any time what is an unreasonable request. I can also deal with the consequences of changing my mind about a previously agreed upon request.

❋

WHAT IF . . .

MY CHILDREN DON'T LISTEN TO ME?

Then I can take stock of how and when I approach them. I can try to see our situation from their views and see what is bugging them. I can talk to others about how they reach their children.

—and—

I can examine my expectations of them and of myself. I can set realistic expectations for each of my children and ask their help with this. I can look at the times when my children are listening a little bit better, and see what it is I am doing that is helping. I can watch for these times when they are listening a little better, and I can ask them "What is it I do that makes you want to listen to me?"

❋

If my children don't listen to me, I have the ability to correct the situation.

61

❊

WHAT IF . . .

I LOST ALL THE WEIGHT I THOUGHT I SHOULD LOSE?

Then the way I looked at myself and what I thought of myself would probably change. If that changed, then I would also act differently. I may have to deal with envy from others. I would have to give up poor eating habits that tended to feel good. I would have to find other ways to feel good.

—*and*—

I would have to begin a new lifestyle that included new patterns of eating and exercise. I might need to ask others around me to help me maintain the new lifestyle. I would have to make the new ways into regular habits over time.

❊

A change in the way I look affects other parts of me. I can choose to make this change work for me.

MARCH

I am hungry for my power
not for control
but to remember
who I am
who I came here to be
and
what I am to do

WHAT IF . . .

I HAVE TO MOVE OUT OF MY HOME IN MY OLD AGE?

Then this would be a major change for me. I have gone through major changes before and I know that discomfort goes along with it. I have moved before. I can prepare ahead of time for this change.

—and—

I can take steps to find an adequate place or I can ask for help from trusted loved ones. I do not have to bear this alone. If I need to, I can decide to learn to live in a new place.

❀

I can use the experience of my past to help me as I face the issues of aging.

❋

WHAT IF . . .

I ACCEPTED MYSELF JUST AS I AM?

Then I would give up the idea that what others think is vitally important. I would listen to the beat of my own drum. I would decide on what is important to me and make sure that happened. I would deal with others' reactions in an accepting way, allowing them a difference of opinion.

—and—

I would choose my own timing and ways—ones that fit me. I would put my own opinion first and take what is useful from what others say. I would guide myself through each situation I faced.

❋

***When I accept myself as I am, I am
confident in guiding my own actions.***

WHAT IF . . .

MY RIGHTS ARE VIOLATED?

Then I will become familiar with the feelings that go along with violation. I may feel anger, hurt and bitterness. I may have other feelings as well. I can handle these feelings if I allow myself to have them. I may deny what hurt me.

—and—

I now have the chance to learn to protect myself in new ways. I will be sure of my boundaries. I will learn what it takes to make me feel safe. I can choose to address the violation. Gradually, protecting myself will become habit.

❀

When my rights are violated, I learn new ways to protect myself. Protecting myself can become a useful habit.

❀

WHAT IF . . .

THERE IS NO WAY TO GET WHAT I WANT?

Then I may feel hopeless or helpless or both. I may ask "Why me?" I may also need to look at what I am trying to get and see if it's really what I want. Or I may have to look at why I gave up trying.

—and—

When I look inside I learn more about me— what I want, what I am willing to do to get it, what is really important to me, what I have done to get what I want. All of these are lessons about me.

❀

I can learn what I need to do next from looking at the times I feel hopeless and helpless.

❀

WHAT IF . . .

I HELPED OTHERS TOO MUCH?

Then I would feel useful only by what I did for them. I would get meaning in my life from how often I extended my energy to others. I might often feel ovewhelmed. I might put great weight on what others think of me and be at the mercy of their approval.

—and—

I might also learn what my limits are through trial and error. I may be able to see that by doing too much for others, I am keeping them from learning on their own. If I choose to learn when to step back, others can learn what they need to learn in their own ways.

❀

Helping others too much may lead me to see that I need to learn to set my own limits.

❀

WHAT IF . . .

I OFTEN MADE A POINT TO CHECK IN WITH MYSELF ON HOW I FEEL?

Then at first this might wear me out. I might not know how I feel about something initially. I might have to take time to sort out my feelings. I might have to come up with a name for how I feel.

—and—

When I figure out how I feel about something, then I am faced with the decision of what to do with my feelings. I am faced with figuring out a way to honor my feelings and take care of them.

❀

When I check on my own feelings, I am learning to honor what I feel and to find ways to take care of myself.

WHAT IF . . .

OTHERS THINK THAT WHAT I AM DOING IS A WASTE OF MY TIME AND TALENT?

Then I will feel the pang of their criticism or disapproval. I will have to compare their opinions with my own and see which one I value most. I may lose some friends or support over the decision I make.

—and—

I can think about their opinions and decide if they are correct. I can give myself time to look at my choices or I can choose to back up my choices. Either way, the only person I need answer to is myself.

❀

I know enough to make good choices and deal with disapproval from others.

❧

WHAT IF . . .

THERE'S A LOT TO DO AND EVERYONE THINKS I OUGHT TO BE DOING IT?

Then I will feel the pressure of both the amount of work and the requests to do the work. I may feel persuaded to take on more than my limits allow. I may allow myself to be talked into doing others' work. I may end up resentful and overwhelmed.

—and—

I have the chance to figure out what my limits are and present what I can do to the group. I can back up my decision by refusing to take on any more than this. I can say to the group, "Here is what I am able to do at this time. . . ."

❧

***I will not take on any more
than I can handle.***

❀

WHAT IF . . .

I HAVE NO FREE TIME?

Then I can look at what I have asked myself to do. Is my schedule rigid? Have I scheduled too much? Do I have the habit of scheduling too many things? If I had free time, would I fill it with responsibilities? Do I blame loved ones for the lack of free time in my life?

—and—

What would I choose to do if I had regular free time? Could I stand to do nothing once in a while? Could I really relax? If I relaxed, would I just fall asleep out of exhaustion? If I were enjoying free time, what would I see myself doing?

❀

Unscheduled time is a healthy part of my life.

❀

WHAT IF . . .

I GET CAUGHT IN TRAFFIC?

Then I will likely arrive later than I expected. I may feel like I owe others an explanation. I may feel panicky and work extra hard to drive very fast the rest of the way. I may blame others for the traffic and wish them ill.

—and—

I also have the opportunity to tell myself to relax. In those moments I can breathe deeply. I can encourage myself to take my time. I can tell myself that being late is part of life; it happens from time to time. I can refuse to be driven by circumstances beyond my control.

❀

In any heavy traffic, I can calm my mind and still my actions.

WHAT IF . . .

I HAD FEWER FRIENDS?

Then I may feel a little more lonely from time to time. I may miss the parts others have played in my life. I may also have to deal with the time left on my hands when some of my friends no longer fill my time.

—and—

I may find some very interesting parts of myself that I didn't know existed. I may examine the qualities of a good friend and appreciate the friends that are still in my life. I may have more time to accomplish my own goals.

❀

I can recognize true friendship and appreciate its place in my life.

❀

WHAT IF . . .

I FORGET TO ASK MYSELF WHAT I NEED IN ANY NEW SITUATION?

Then I will force others to decide things for me that I could be deciding for myself. I will be helping them to assume they know what I need and that they do not need to consult me.

—and—

I may be forced to accept less than what I need or want. I can begin the habit of checking with myself in any new situation. Once I know my needs, I can choose to take this position: "What I need right now is . . ."

❀

Entering a new situation can serve as my clue to take time to figure out what I need.

WHAT IF . . .

THEY TELL ME I AM STUPID?

Then I will be in a situation where I may choose to feel stupid. I may find myself wanting to accept their assessment of me, especially if I have done this before. I may continue a habit of accepting others' opinions of myself.

—and—

I also have the chance to challenge their opinion *and* my habit of accepting others' views of me. I can choose to rethink what I am doing or I can decide that what I am doing is what is best. I can decide to ignore someone's opinion and give real value to my own.

❀

Someone's negative ideas about me offer me the chance to value my own opinion.

❀

WHAT IF . . .

THEY ACT LIKE MY OPINIONS DON'T COUNT?

Then I am likely to feel ignored and overlooked. I may feel hurt and say, "What's wrong with me?" I may feel my views are unimportant and ignore my own opinions as others do. I am likely to feel sad and bitter.

—and—

Instead I can stand my ground. I can treat my opinions with great importance. I can offer them no matter what the reaction. I can decide that others' reactions do not determine my actions. I can stand behind what I believe.

❀

I choose to honor my opinions and stand behind them with my actions.

WHAT IF . . .

I HAVE TO PAY MORE TAXES THAN I THOUGHT?

Then I may be forced to rethink my financial situation. I may have to come up with ways to make more money or ways to cut spending. I may have to dream up a payment arrangement that is acceptable to the other party. I will find out what it takes to cooperate with those in power.

—and—

I have the chance to take responsibility for my actions and rethink my ways with money. I have the chance to learn how to solve a problem by negotiating a way to pay what I owe.

❀

I am able to take care of tax problems using skills that have worked for me in the past.

❀

WHAT IF . . .

I DON'T KNOW WHAT TO DO WHEN I AM SAD?

Then I might feel lost, especially if I am prone to think that I ought to *do* something. I may try things that cover up the sadness or make it feel as if it has gone away. Or I may want to run from it. I have many choices.

—and—

I can choose to see sadness as a normal part of life and human experience. I can choose to do nothing and just let my sadness run its course. Or I can feel my sadness and act upon my feelings as they arise. Expressing my sadness in a safe way is a healthy thing to do. I may ask for help.

❀

When I honor my feelings of sadness, I allow myself to be truly human.

WHAT IF . . .

IT RAINS AT THE WRONG TIME?

Then I may be forced to change my plans. I may feel very inconvenienced or even irritated. My ability to think creatively about solutions may be temporarily stopped.

—and—

I can allow myself to feel upset about this for as long as I need. Then I can think about what the alternatives are in my situation. I can make plans for other activities that do not depend on the weather. I can look at my options in any situation that is beyond my control.

❦

I am directed by my own ability to think creatively for solutions in situations beyond my control.

❀

WHAT IF . . .

WE HAVE TO ADD MORE PAPERWORK AT THE OFFICE?

Then I am likely to feel put out, put upon and resentful. I may demonstrate my complaints in my behavior by refusing to comply.

—and—

I am also presented with the opportunity to re-organize my ways more usefully. I can take the new paperwork and reorganize it in a more efficient way. Or I can choose to state my complaints in a manner that reflects well on me and takes into account my needs.

❀

I can present my complaints and organize my ways in a manner that represents me well.

❖

WHAT IF . . .

I HAVE TO WAIT A LONG TIME FOR AN ANSWER?

Then I may feel angry and impatient or even bitter. I may blame others or my Higher Power for the long wait. I may use the time waiting to compare my lack to others' surplus. I may develop envy or jealousy.

—and—

I can choose to use the time of waiting to figure out what I have to do to be patient. I can take interest in my affairs and become very good at handling them. I can also practice my faith while I wait for an answer.

❖

What I do with the time that I am asked to wait for an answer is up to me.

❀

WHAT IF . . .

I HAVE TO GIVE UP MY CHILDREN?

Then I will likely feel devastated, or as if my world is over. I may feel extremely lonely. I may feel that I am not now nor could I ever be a good parent. I may fret constantly over what my children think of me and what is happening to them.

—and—

I may take the time away from them to see if there are things I need to work on or do differently. I can look at things I need to change and get the help I need to change them. I can allow myself to learn from the areas where I need improvement. I can learn to handle my own emotions around this loss.

❀

I can use time away from my children to improve upon myself as a person.

❀

WHAT IF . . .

I CAME TO BELIEVE THAT EVERYONE IS SACRED?

Then I would have to give up all the old ideas about myself that don't fit the idea of "sacred." It might be hard to let them go. I would have to trade negative ideas I have about myself and others for ideas that honor me and them.

—and—

I may experience some sadness in letting these ideas go. If I see myself and others as sacred, then I will have to learn to treat all of us this way in my actions, thoughts and feelings. I will have to lose old habits and begin new ones that are healthy.

❀

As I hold myself and others in high regard, I change my habits to fit my beliefs.

❀

WHAT IF . . .

MY KIDS DON'T DO THEIR SHARE?

Then I can try to determine where they got the idea that this was alright with me. I can ask myself what part I have in their understanding of responsibility. I can also ask myself if I need to change in order to help them change.

—and—

I now have the chance to show them a new way of what I expect and how to comply with my request. I can ask for their help with this and our relationship can develop a more cooperative tone than we've had in the past.

❀

At any time I can try different ways to get the cooperation of my kids.

WHAT IF . . .

I MET THE LOVE OF MY LIFE?

Then I would be in the position of making a decision about what to do with that love. I might feel I need to run from it or insist that it last forever. Or I might test it to see if it is real or just doubt it from the moment it begins.

—and—

I also have the chance for some happiness and fulfillment. I can choose to walk this road and find out what each moment brings. I can see the ups and downs as normal for love relationships. I can let myself have this gift and tell myself "I deserve it." I can fully experience the love for each moment I am allowed to have it.

❀

***I can choose to fully experience
the love of my life.***

❀

WHAT IF . . .

I WORKED ON MY HOPES AND DREAMS?

Then it might mean I would have to leave the business of the world around me. It might mean that I would have to break new ground. I might venture into the unknown and feel very scared of what I find there. I might have to rely on my wits to provide for my needs. I might have to give up the security of others' control over parts of my life.

—and—

Working on my hopes and dreams may mean I find a new inner strength and a new meaning for myself. I may find what is natural to me in work and in relationships. I may find that when I work on hopes and dreams, the power of the universe gets behind me as a resource.

❀

***Working on my hopes and dreams
draws out my natural strength, talent
and ability. The power of the universe
gets behind me to help.***

WHAT IF . . .

OTHERS SAY I AM SELFISH?

Then I may have given them the idea that I will *always* put myself first. I may be acting differently towards them than they are used to, and I may choose to explain my new behavior. I may have to deal with their own selfish attitudes about how I spend my time.

—and—

I can also evaluate my behavior to see if I think it is selfish. I can ask myself this question without fear of the answer. I can always make the changes I see that need to be made. I can determine my part in any problem and the parts of others in the problem.

❀

I can trust myself to determine my part in any problem I have.

❀

WHAT IF . . .

EVERYONE GIVES UP ON ME?

Then I may feel abandoned or lonely or angry. I may feel that I cannot do what I need to do without support. I may feel like I am wrong and they are right. I may consider or actually abandon what I am doing.

—and—

I can decide to support myself. I can refuse to give up on myself. I can decide that what I am doing fits me and no one else has to understand this. I can choose to confront the ones who have given up on me or I can choose to put my energy into what I want to do. I can consider that others are acting out their envy because they are unwilling to test their own limits. I can live with the consequences of my actions.

❀

No matter what others do, I can choose to support my attitudes in any situation.

WHAT IF . . .

I TOOK CARE OF MY INNER CHILD?

Then I might be very busy trying to understand the needs of my child within. I might have to do some detective work to figure out what those needs are and how to best meet them. I might find many hurt places within that still need a parent. I might feel overwhelmed with the work I see that needs doing.

—and—

In learning to do this work, I may feel for the first time that my needs are real and that they count. I may be the first person that ever took those needs seriously. I can try different ways to meet those needs. Maybe for the first time, I will feel love for myself.

❀

***Paying attention to my inner child
means that my needs will be
taken seriously.***

❀

WHAT IF . . .

I AM IN TOO MUCH PAIN TO THINK CLEARLY?

Then I may be forced to stop thinking about my situation for a while. Or I may have to give up trying to change the current situation and begin accepting what is happening to me.

—and—

I can take a rest from trying to solve everything by thinking. I can open myself to answers that come in other ways. I can learn to wait and use the waiting period to rest from my usual approach that causes me pain.

❀

In painful times I can trust myself to wait for answers in new ways. I can rest from having to solve it all.

WHAT IF . . .

I WANTED TO LEAVE MY RELATIONSHIP?

Then I might review my reasons repeatedly to see what is in my best interest. Such a review may cause some extreme pain and anxiety. I might have to plan an escape, confront my partner or face the possibility of loss or a bad decision.

—and—

Wanting to leave a relationship may mean that I should take another look at what I need in my life right now. It may also mean asking my partner for help so that my needs are met whether I am in the relationship or not. I may also have to deal with the fear of being alone and looking inside myself and to others for strength.

❧

Wanting to leave my relationship opens the door for me to examine what I really need and then to do something about it.

❀

WHAT IF . . .

THE JOY GOES OUT OF MY LIFE?

Then I will feel the opposite of joy. I will likely feel sorrow. I may feel really uncomfortable with the power of this emotion. I may feel that sorrow is an unnatural state. I may feel as if it could consume me. I may think I will not find happiness again. I may find ways to cover up this sorrow or to deny it.

—and—

This is a clue for me to see what has caused the sorrow. I can ask myself what was I doing when I felt joy. I can also ask myself who supports me in my pursuit of what gives me joy. I can look around me to see if the support I need is available. I can support myself by taking my feelings seriously and seeing if I need to do something different to help myself at this time. I can also choose to sit with my sorrow for as long as that feels right to me.

❀

Joy and sorrow are natural parts of my life. I accept them both.

❀

WHAT IF . . .

MY PARENTS HAD SUPPORTED THE THINGS I WANTED TO DO?

Then perhaps it would be easier for me to do new things and try new ways. It could also leave me thinking that I could try all the things I wanted with no thought of commitment and stability. I could expect that all others I meet would do the same for me as my parents did.

—and—

I can choose to see that what my parents did with me was what they could do at the time with the knowledge they had. I can acknowledge any suffering that I endured because of their ways with me. I can choose if and how my parents will be a part of my life. Now I can make sure that I take my own needs seriously.

❀

I can provide the support I now need for any task I choose. I can use my parents' example of support to show me how to support myself or I can improve on their ways.

APPRIL

i am hungry
for my power
not for control
but to remember
who i am
who i came here to be
and what i am to do

i am hungry
for faith in me
that moves me to action

WHAT IF . . .

EVERYONE THOUGHT I ABANDONED THEM?

Then I am likely to meet with cries for my help and disapproval and hurt from others. I am likely to feel defensive and may want to explain away what I am doing. I may be less than eager to allow others their feelings.

—and—

I can let them have their feelings. I can have a different sense of what I am doing than what they think. I can choose to explain my actions. I can try to see how they feel. Still, I can have my own reaction. I can change when it suits me and in response to demands most suitable to me.

❊

I do what I need to do, and I let others have their feelings.

❊

WHAT IF . . .

I REALLY USED MY TALENTS?

Then my life would be different. Do I even know what my talents are? I am wondering if I would be happier. I may also have to stop some of the habits I have now. I would be faced with decisions about how to best spend my time. I might have to make some major changes. I might have to learn new skills to develop my talents.

—and—

I would be dealing with others reactions, both positive and negative, to what I produced. I might get more satisfaction from what I do. I may feel a deep sense of joy in whatever I do.

❊

***In using my talents, I learn new skills
and feel satisfaction.***

❋

WHAT IF . . .

I WAS THE ONLY WHO BELIEVED IN MY DREAM?

Then I would probably feel it doesn't have much life. I might begin to think that it is worthless. I might give it up to do something that would get more approval from others. I may give it up altogether.

—and—

I may choose to see if my dream can come to life. I may decide my dream is part of my purpose in life and that I must see the outcome of trying to make it real. I may choose to talk myself into trying, even when no one else thinks it will work.

❋

The support I give myself for my dream gives me enough energy to get started.

WHAT IF . . .

THEY CHANGE THE SUBJECT WHEN I AM SAYING SOMETHING THAT IS IMPORTANT TO ME?

Then I will likely feel cut off, and I may think that what I have to say is not important. I may agree with them that I wasn't speaking and that my ideas are not worth hearing. I may decide that it is "safer" to be quiet.

—and—

I can decide whether I will confront them or not. I can also decide if I want to continue conversing or not. I can choose to use my energy elsewhere for my own purposes. If I choose to confront them, I can state what I have to say. If I am interrupted, I can look at the speaker who did so and say, "I will finish what I am saying now."

❀

I am not controlled by others' reactions in conversations. I decide when and how I want to spend my energy in conversation.

❀

WHAT IF . . .

NO ONE SEES HOW HARD
I AM TRYING?

Then I may feel hurt and overlooked. I may try to convince others of my hard work and they still may not see it. I may try even harder and end up overworking myself. I may quit if I do not get the approval I think I need.

—and—

If no one sees my efforts it is time for me to take note and appreciate them myself. I can also figure out what makes me feel outside approval is so important. I can decide if outside approval needs to remain that important or if I need to pay more attention to approval of my own work.

❀

I can choose to approve of my own work and let others' opinions of it take backseat to my approval.

❈

WHAT IF . . .

MY WORK WAS HONORED BY MANY?

Then I would be dealing with others' opinions of me on a regular basis. I would need to learn to value my own opinion first and not let others' reactions take priority over my own. I would have to learn to deal with praise and being in the limelight.

—and—

This would give me the chance to remain focused on the work itself and not on others' reactions to it. I would have to work on ways to concentrate my efforts so that my job gets done. I may have to draw some new boundaries so that I, not others, structure my time. I would have to learn to accept compliments on work well done.

❈

When my work is honored it offers me the opportunity to accept compliments and remained focused on my work.

❀

WHAT IF . . .

I FORGET SOME USEFUL INFORMATION?

Then I may temporarily be frustrated or embarrassed. I may have to repeat some previous efforts to find the information. Waiting for the information may cause an inconvenience to myself or to others.

—and—

In gathering the same information twice, I may pick up on something new. I may have to give up the idea of perfection as I offer information to others. When I allow myself not to know everything, I become more human and gentle with myself.

❀

I can use and offer information in the way it comes to me.

❧

WHAT IF . . .

I DIE ALONE?

Then I can realize that most people die alone. Few people die alongside anyone else. I can ask myself what issues this brings to mind for me. What are the important things in my life that remain unresolved? If I think about dying alone, I can imagine the feelings I will have and deal with them now.

—and—

I have the chance to resolve for myself what I think happens when we die. I can think about this before I die and come to terms with it. I can now take stock of my life, make needed changes and be grateful for all I have. I can even imagine how I would like to die.

❧

I can look at my own death, determine what I need to finish before then and make plans that will suit me personally.

❦

WHAT IF . . .

I WORK TOO HARD AND MY HEALTH SUFFERS?

Then the state of my health is my cue to change my work habits. I may have to work less, accept less pay, take a different job or ask for some relief. Each of these arrangements can cause me some discomfort. I can ask myself how much I value my own health.

—and—

Once I know the value of my own health, I can outline the steps I need to take to secure the level of health I find acceptable. I can restructure my work to support my idea of good health. I can ask others to help me as I begin healthier, new habits.

❦

I choose new habits of good health that suit me. I can change my life to achieve a healthier lifestyle.

❋

WHAT IF . . .

EVERYONE GETS THE WRONG IDEA ABOUT ME?

Then in their presence, I will probably feel some discomfort. I will feel that their reactions to me are strange and make little sense. My energy could easily get tied up in their ideas instead of where I want it to be.

—and—

I can choose to confront those persons whose ideas about me are wrong or I can ignore their reactions. Or I can look at my own actions to see if I contributed to their wrong ideas about me. Or I can let them have their ideas, right or wrong, and focus on whatever interests me instead.

❋

When others have the wrong idea about me, I can choose the right action that best suits me.

❦

WHAT IF . . .

I BEGAN TO LOVE WHAT IS
IN MY HEART?

Then I would have to stop all the hurtful things I think, say and feel about myself. I would replace these with kind thoughts and feelings that match the love. I would have to learn to love all that I find in my heart, including all the wounds I have suffered and the sorrows I have faced.

—and—

In loving all I find in my heart, I can become more fully human and more fully alive. I can become more accepting of myself. I can pay more attention to my needs, take care of them and accept my own efforts. I can quit expecting others to take care of me and do the job well myself.

❦

Loving all that I find in my heart shows me how to take care of myself.

❁

WHAT IF . . .

I CAN'T PROTECT MY CHILDREN FROM HARM?

Then I am likely to fret over the outcomes they face in their lives. Taken to an extreme this could become the central focus in my life. I could lose all interest in what fascinates me. If I try too hard, my children may feel smothered.

—and—

I can choose to show them ways to protect themselves and support them for doing it themselves. I can offer a helpful ear for their troubles. I can step back and let them solve their troubles so they can learn from them. I can get out of their way and let them stumble onto the ways that make sense to them. I can look at the issue of personal faith in my life and how it works to help me address their safety.

❁

The faith I have helps me look at how I deal with my children's safety.

❀

WHAT IF . . .

OTHERS WANT ME TO ANSWER FOR MY ACTIONS AND I DON'T WANT TO DO IT?

Then there will be a clash between us. I may be uncomfortable with the conflict and may want to run from it. I may deny that the conflict exists or I may try to address the issues with those on the other side.

—and—

I have the chance to decide how I want to support what is important to me. I may decide that I will not answer to anyone for my actions, and I will accept the consequences of that decision. If I decide to answer to others for my actions, I can plan what I will say so that I can state my case well. I support my opinion of my own actions.

❀

I make good decisions about when and how I answer for my actions.

❀

WHAT IF . . .

MY LOVED ONE IS AFRAID TO GO FOR MEDICAL HELP?

Then I have to decide whether I must force the issue or respect the opinion of my loved one. I can fight with her/him over this or I can help search for the underlying reason(s) that lead to the fear of getting help. I may end up frustrated with the outcome or fear the loss of the loved one.

—and—

I have the opportunity to draw closer to my loved one, know him/her on a deeper level and understand the decision to go or not to go. I can also search my own heart for what troubles me most and what moves me to want to control the outcome for my loved one. I can benefit from looking at my reaction to the fear of losing someone. I can examine issues of personal faith and let these help me.

❀

I can become closer to my loved one and work on my fear of losing someone I love.

❀

WHAT IF . . .

THE WAY WAS MADE CLEAR FOR ME TO DO WHAT I WANT?

Then I would probably have to make quick changes in my life. I might be shocked that I could actually do what I want. I might need a push to get started, especially if I always had to work hard for things in the past. I might have to gather my self-confidence.

—and—

I would have the responsibility to make what I want happen, to charge ahead with the dream and make decisions along the way that support it. I might find myself more connected and responsible to the resourcefulness of the universe. Quite simply, if the way was made clear for what I wanted to do, then I have no reason to refuse to do it.

❀

If I tell myself the way is clear, then I can move ahead with what I want to do.

❀

WHAT IF . . .

I HAD A GOOD DAY?

Then I might have to admit that it's possible to have one. I might have another one. I might notice from this that I pay more attention to what goes wrong than I do to what goes right in my life.

—and—

Noticing what goes right takes practice. Am I willing to look at what goes right or what I enjoy? I will notice also that paying attention to what goes well also invites me to be grateful.

❀

Gratitude is the state of mind that comes from paying attention to what goes right in my life.

❀

WHAT IF . . .

I LET GO OF RESPONSIBILITY FOR OTHERS' REACTIONS?

Then immediately I might feel less important in their lives and less involved with them. I might feel less central in the lives of all those around me; my role with them would change. Discomfort and an unsettling sense of "What do I do now?" comes with change. I may feel a sense of loss.

—and—

I will have more, maybe a lot more time on my hands to put toward something else. I can study my own reactions and let others have theirs. I can let go of the burden of having to keep everyone happy or know their moods. Then I am faced with new choices about what to do with the time I once devoted to others' reactions.

❀

If I am more focused on my own reactions, I open up possibilities for exciting uses of my time.

❧

WHAT IF . . .

THERE IS NOT ENOUGH TIME, MONEY AND LOVE?

Then I feel insecure, as if I must grab what I can when I can get it. I must crush others or be jealous of their dreams and achievements because there is not enough time, money and love to go around.

—and—

I can also decide where my idea of "not having enough" came from. What needs did I lack earlier in my life? I can look at ways to meet those needs now. Jealousy is a clue to my lack of something. I can help myself decide if this lack also applies to my ability to take care of myself now.

❧

I can challenge each lack in my life as it comes up for me.

❀

WHAT IF . . .

I ACCEPT MY FAMILY MEMBERS FOR WHO THEY ARE?

Then I will have to let go of any expectations they will change. I will have to also let go of the idea that we should all be alike or that we have to be close. I may have to let go of the idea that I still need a mommy or a daddy. I may feel a real loss or I may feel like an orphan.

—and—

If I free my family members from my expectations of them, then they can no longer disappoint me. The kind of relationship that I can have with them will become more clear. I can let go of past resentments. I can choose if my family members are a part of my life today.

❀

Accepting family members for who they are frees me from disappointment, resentment and waiting for others to change.

❀

WHAT IF . . .

I EXAMINED MY THOUGHTS TO SEE HOW THEY AFFECT MY FEELINGS?

Then I would learn to trace each feeling back to a thought that went before it, which takes practice and commitment. I would likely find some thoughts that lead to bad feelings. I would see that I thought I was unworthy or unlikable or deficient in some way.

—and—

Then I could attack the thoughts to see where they came from or how I got the idea. I would have to challenge the thoughts to see if I really believed them or if I had talked myself into believing these things about myself. I might have to recognize what's at the core of this belief I have about myself.

❀

I can examine my thoughts to see how they affect my feelings. I can find my core beliefs that need to be challenged.

❈

WHAT IF . . .

OTHERS BLAME ME FOR THEIR PARTS IN A PROBLEM SITUATION?

Then I am stuck in the middle, needing to respond and probably feeling defensive. I will likely feel pressured, and I'll want to strike back at those who blame me.

—and—

I can make choices about their blame. I can allow them their feelings without agreeing with them. I can tell myself that they have a right to their feelings and so do I. I can choose to accept the blame or I can take this opportunity to know what my role is with the problem. I am responsible for knowing only my role and taking whatever stand I need to protect it.

❈

I see my part in any given problem and only accept responsiblity for that.

❈

WHAT IF . . .

EVERYONE AROUND ME THINKS WHAT I AM DOING IS CRAZY?

Then I will likely feel surrounded by doubt and discouraging energy. I may feel a sense of betrayal if my loved ones see my actions as bizarre. I may feel very threatened and lose sight of what is important to me.

—*and*—

I can regain sight of what is important to me by looking at my own actions to see if they're supported or ridiculed. I can look for areas where I need to make changes. I can decide if I need to confront the others or let them think what they will. If I confront them or not, I need to remember what is important to me. If I take care of what is important to me, then I am taking care of me.

❈

When discouraged by others' reactions, I see what I need to change and keep what is important to me.

WHAT IF . . .

I AM LATE FOR WORK?

Then work will start without me on this day. I may feel uncomfortable or threatened by not being there. I may rush to get there and end up hurting myself or someone else. I can get into a bad mood that only makes matters worse when I do get to work.

—and—

I can say to myself, "Today I will be late." I can allow myself to make the error and move on. I can be directed by a sense of responsible behavior rather than the ticking of the clock. I can take responsibility for the act of being late, knowing that this happens to everyone from time to time.

❀

I own my behavior and the feelings I have about it.

&

WHAT IF . . .

I CHOOSE MY PRINCIPLES OVER OTHERS' IDEAS OF WHAT I SHOULD BE DOING?

Then I may be in for a lonely walk. I may see others flee in the heat of debate or take a more popular side. I may be asked harsh questions about my stand or I may be ridiculed.

—and—

I can see that I have a stage to stand on for the principles I uphold. People who question or ridicule me are waiting for a response. I have a few minutes to offer them another view of an issue while they are still open to debate. I gain a sense of peace from honoring the principles I believe in.

&

I can tolerate questions about my principles since it gives me a chance to stand up for them.

❀

WHAT IF . . .

MY PARENTS DISAPPROVE
OF WHAT I AM DOING?

Then I may feel very uncomfortable with the
roles they think that they have in my life. I may
feel as though they violate my space, intruding
whenever they want to. I may react to them like
a spoiled child, which tells them that I really do
need their help. I may see the need to redefine
the boundaries between us.

—and—

I can look at the role I have let my parents play
in my life up to this point. I can see what areas
need changing. I can examine where I've let
them help me when I could have helped myself.
Right action includes taking care of my needs in
an adult fashion and telling them what I want so
that they can clearly understand it.

❀

*I can determine my needs, fill them, and
allow my parents to step back from me.*

❀

WHAT IF . . .

THEY MAKE FUN OF MY IDEAS?

Then, at first, I will feel awkward and ill at ease. I may feel the need to defend my ideas or explain my reasons and choices. I may stop talking or contributing to others if my ideas are not readily accepted.

—and—

I can look at what I think is behind their laughter, such as their own insecurity, jealousy or envy. There are many more possibilities other than that my ideas are odd in some way. I can decide that I will stand behind my ideas and keep presenting them. I may also choose to confront those who laugh or I may choose to ignore their actions. I have many choices in how I respond.

❀

I choose to support my ideas no matter what kind of reactions I receive.

❁

WHAT IF . . .

I WANT TO WORK FOR MYSELF AND DON'T KNOW HOW?

Then I may think that there is no way to accomplish this. I may shut down the good ideas I have and go to work for someone else. I may turn my back on a dream of mine and replace it with someone else's project.

—and—

I now have the choice to find out what it takes to work for myself. I can find out what I need to know by asking questions from different sources about self-employment information. I can talk to others who work for themselves. I can retrieve my dream while I work for someone else or I can venture out on my own. I can do this one step at a time.

❁

I feed my dreams with hope and support them with my actions.

❀

WHAT IF . . .

I MOVED MOUNTAINS OF DISBELIEF WITH MY FAITH?

Then I would have to acknowledge the power of faith in my life. I would see what can be accomplished when I apply faith and action. I would completely let go of fear. I may be a little shocked or in disbelief. I may require reassurance.

—and—

I would act to make the goals I have set come true. I could outline the exact steps I need to take. I would feel myself fill with joy. I would experience a "high" from exercising my faith and feel compelled to share it with others.

❀

If I choose to move the mountains of disbelief in my life, I will be filled with joy.

====== ❁ ======

WHAT IF . . .

I RECOGNIZE THE INFLUENCE I HAVE ON OTHERS?

Then I must examine how I use this power. I may feel more entitled to their regard than I actually am. I may put myself on a pedestal. I may also fall off that same pedestal.

—and—

If I see the influence I have on others, then I can choose to use it wisely. I can ask myself how best I can represent myself and serve others as well. I can grow from studying what I want to do with the influential position I have been given. I can look at my intentions and my actions. I can move ahead based on inner principles that guide right action.

❁

If I am placed in an influential position, I need to study the best way to use this power and guide my actions.

❧

WHAT IF . . .

I SAW MYSELF AS UNIQUE?

Then I would give up the need to conform to all the opinions of others. I could find the right path that draws out my talents. I would acknowledge my talents and abilities and be grateful for them. I would give up the idea that everyone has to do what I do or think what I think. I would give up trying to reach that outcome.

—and—

I would very likely see others as unique. I would recognize and appreciate what it is in them that makes them unique. Like candles burning in the darkness, I would see lights glowing everywhere. Though each light is made from the same thing, each burns in a slightly different way and none diminish any other.

❧

Seeing myself and others as unique creative expressions keeps me grateful.

MAY

i am hungry
for my power
not for control
but to remember
who i am
who i came here to be
and what i am to do

i am hungry
for faith in me
that moves me to action

i am hungry
to feed on my birthright

i can feed on
faith in myself
one act
after another

❀

WHAT IF . . .

MY FAMILY DOES NOT APPROVE OF MY PARTNER?

Then I will be faced with a decision of prioritizing my relationships. I may be asked to take sides or I may find myself separated from my family. I may struggle with influence from my family and my partner.

—and—

I also have the chance to be in the relationship I choose for myself and to let my family be only as close as I want them to be. I have the chance to be supported by my partner as I show my family how I want to be treated. I am not locked into any role or certain way to handle things. My family may learn new ways by the stand I take.

❀

I can choose the role I want for myself with both my partner and my family.

WHAT IF . . .

MY PARENTS DO NOT APPROVE OF
THE WORK I DO?

Then I may feel criticized and degraded. I may be doing the opposite of what I think they wanted me to do. I may respond to them in spiteful ways or feel bitter toward them. I may get separated from my own dreams as I chase away their criticism.

—and—

I can choose to limit how much I let their ideas influence what I do. I can also limit the amount of time I spend with the negative influences I receive from them. I can tell them I'll consider their ideas, yet still continue to do the kind of work I want to do.

❊

When parents or others criticize my choices, I can still decide to choose what fits me well.

❀

WHAT IF . . .

I REALIZED THAT I COULD CREATE MY LIFE AS I WANTED TO EACH DAY?

Then I would know that I was responsible for my decisions and I would put great thought into every day. I would probably give up complaining about the events in my life.

—and—

I would see how my thoughts influence my actions. I would feel gratitude more often, and I would choose what supports my higher good.

❀

Creating my life each day leads me to gratitude and supports my higher good.

❀

WHAT IF . . .

THERE ARE NO OPPORTUNITIES OPEN TO ME NOW?

Then I may feel overlooked or left out. I may resent others who do have these opportunities. I may shut myself off to other opportunities that are available. I may choose self-pity as a way to cope.

—*and*—

Just as easily I can look for other doors that are open for me. I can explore what is behind these doors. I can choose to trust that I will find something that suits me or that I will be given a new understanding of my situation.

If doors close for me I can find others that are open for my exploration.

❀

WHAT IF . . .

I COULD KEEP MY SENSE OF PERSONAL POWER?

Then I would have the responsibility of using it well. I would have to decide what "wise use" means. I would also have to deal with others' reactions to my use of power. These reactions may include jealousy and envy.

—and—

If I choose to look at what "wise use" means to me, then I can explore my personal purpose and use my power for the greatest good. I can generate the solutions I need to deal with others' negative reactions.

❀

I can determine how to keep my personal power and how to react to others.

❊

WHAT IF . . .

SOMEONE TRIES TO TAKE MY PARTNER FROM ME?

Then I have to examine my own issues of trust. I have to see if I have a problem with trust or if there is a serious problem in my relationship. I may find that it is both. Either way, I am faced with choosing to make myself more comfortable.

—and—

I can choose to get my partner's help to understand how he/she sees my trust issues. I can explore the causes of any problems I have about trust with a counselor. With my partner I can explore the affect these problems have on our relationship.

❊

I can look at my issues of trust to see if changes need to be made in me or in my relationship.

WHAT IF . . .

I DISAPPOINT THOSE CLOSE TO ME?

Then I may be asked to look at others' expectations of me to see if they are out of my reach. I can also choose to look at my own expectations of myself and see if I am expecting reasonable behavior with consideration of my circumstances.

—and—

I could look at the situation causing disappointment to see if I let others' reactions control me in any way. I can recognize that some disappointment is, in fact, normal.

❀

I determine how I want to respond to others' disappointment in me.

————— ❀ —————

WHAT IF . . .

I CAN'T FIGURE OUT MY PART IN A PROBLEM FROM SOMEONE ELSE'S PART IN THE PROBLEM?

Then I may need to look at how I assign responsibility for what happens in situations that include me. I may need to discuss this with an objective third party. I can watch for a pattern in my actions that leads to this confusion.

—and—

I can realize that it may be difficult for me to take responsibility for my own actions. I can refuse to assume responsibility for others' actions. I can refuse to assign blame or responsibility until I have time to sort this out.

❀

Taking responsibility for my own actions is important for my health and my relationships.

❀

WHAT IF . . .

I AM LISTENING AND I STILL DO NOT UNDERSTAND?

Then I may feel stupid and want to withdraw from the situation. I may want to leave the scene or I may give up on the goal I had set for myself in this situation.

—and—

I can choose to realize that all things will not always make sense to me. I can let some of these things go and forget them. For those things I cannot forget, I can ask for help from someone who knows more about the subject than I do.

❀

I do not have to give up if I don't understand. I can ask for and receive help.

WHAT IF . . .

I CAN'T PLEASE MY TEACHERS?

Then I may feel I am "missing the boat." I may have to admit that I don't understand and then deal with a reaction from my teachers that I don't like. I may be told that "I just don't have what it takes to do the work."

—and—

Then I can still decide if I agree with this opinion of me. I can ask my teachers to help me understand what is expected of me. I can ask the questions I need to ask. If I do not get the help I need, there are others who know how to help me. I only need to find these people.

❊

When I can't please others, I can still decide to view myself in a positive light.

❀

WHAT IF . . .

I AM LEFT ALONE TO DEFEND MYSELF?

Then I may feel like I cannot do it. I may feel all is lost. I may want to give up, withdraw or hurt myself before others can hurt me.

—and—

I can choose to think about looking inside for strength I didn't know I had. I know others have shown much strength in times of great need. I can choose to believe this about me. In times of great need, I can watch for suggestions that arise in me and consider all of them.

❀

In great need, I can rise to meet the situation if I choose to believe I have reserves of strength inside.

❀

WHAT IF . . .

I CHANGE MY GOAL IN THE MIDDLE OF TRYING TO REACH ANOTHER GOAL?

Then I may have to look at how each goal fits with me. I may change goals because one fits better than the other or because I am afraid I can't reach the goal I really want.

—and—

I can grow from examination of conflicting goals. I can decide which goal supports me better and which goal I can more fully support. I can look at the advantages and disadvantages of each. I will know the proper fit for me when I see it.

❀

I see and set a goal that fits me, and I also know when it is time to change.

❋

WHAT IF . . .

THERE IS NO WAY OUT OF MY SITUATION?

Then I may need help to see what I can do in the situation. I may require professional help or outside assistance to look at all the options. Sometimes my only option may be to learn to cope with the situation.

—and—

I may also learn that doing nothing is sometimes better than coming up with something to do. I may learn to wait on others to act, and I may learn a new sense of patience. I may also have to give up on my situation and leave it to personal faith.

❋

I can live through "no way out" situations.

❀

What if . . .

NO ONE WILL SPEAK UP ABOUT A PROBLEM THEY ALL HAVE?

Then I may feel pushed into a position where I feel I should speak up. I have to decide if this is a role that I want or if others are using manipulation to get me to speak up for everyone.

—and—

I can take the time I need to figure this out. I can choose to speak for myself only, for the whole group or not at all. I can take the time to see what my responsibility is and what is not mine to handle.

❀

I handle problems that I see only after I consider the role I want for myself.

❁

WHAT IF . . .

I STAND ALONE ON A PARTICULAR ISSUE?

Then I may feel the discomfort of others' close scrutiny of my ideas and opinions. I may wish for some company or try to give in to the group.

—and—

If I choose to stand alone on an issue that is important to me, I will learn what it is like to present my ideas. I will learn what I have to do to support my ideas in front of others who disagree. I can put together a reasonable argument and find evidence that supports my argument.

❁

Standing up for what is important to me teaches me how to support my own ideas in the face of adversity.

❀

WHAT IF . . .

I CAN NEVER FIND THE RIGHT CAREER/JOB FOR ME?

Then I can explore what to do in a number of ways. I can try many jobs to see what I like. I may end up liking the variety, and I may change jobs often enough to keep me interested in my work.

—and—

I may ask for help from a professional who can look at my abilities and interests. I can put together plans for getting other jobs or training that I want.

❀

I give myself the final say on any decision I make about the work I do. I can learn valuable lessons from all the work I do.

❁

WHAT IF . . .

I FOUND THAT I ENJOY LEARNING?

Then I might be shocked that learning what I want to learn is different from all other learning situations. I can learn the power and joy of making my own choices. I can discover what gives me the greatest satisfaction.

—and—

I can take the time I need to discover what I want to do with the time I have. I can make changes all the way through old age.

❁

***I can enjoy learning new things
all my life.***

❀

WHAT IF . . .

THERE IS NO ONE TO LISTEN TO ME WHEN I NEED TO TALK?

Then I may feel abandoned. I may think others do not care and I may come to believe that I have no resources inside me.

—*and*—

I can wait for others to come to my aid or I can look at how I have helped myself in the past with similar situations. Even the smallest bit of help I have given to myself can help me now. By looking at what has worked for me in the past, I can see what may fit the situation I'm in now.

❀

I can still find help in myself, even if others are not there for me.

❀

WHAT IF . . .

I DON'T KNOW WHAT MAKES ME REALLY HAPPY?

Then I may let others influence my choices too much. I may be prone to act without thinking and go along with others' thinking before I have considered all my options. Or I can think about others' choices before I make my own.

—and—

I can learn from their successes and failures. I can take the time I need and get information before I make my choice in any given situation. I can look within for what makes my heart sing. I will know what fits me perfectly when I see it.

❀

I can take time and get information about all my options before I make decisions.

WHAT IF . . .

I CAN'T PAY THE RENT?

Then I will have to examine the options I have about making and spending money. I can look at how I budget and how I spend. Are there any emotional needs attached to my spending habits. I can ask for help to solve the problem. Or I can try to use my own abilities to solve it.

—and—

I can confront the prospect of living without shelter and use that as motivation to make needed changes. I can still make choices that take care of my needs.

❀

I choose to see ways to provide for myself even in very difficult situations.

❀

WHAT IF . . .

THE PEOPLE I BELIEVE IN MAKE BIG MISTAKES?

Then I may feel severely disappointed and lose faith in my own beliefs. I may lose trust in those closest to me and question others who care as well. I may have to trim my expectations of these persons.

—and—

I may also come to see them as human beings and capable of errors—large and small. I can also remember my own errors as evidence that this is a common condition, especially when humans are put on pedestals. I can regain trust over time and with reasonable expectations.

❀

Seeing myself and others as humans allows for trust, error and reasonable expectations.

❄

WHAT IF . . .

THE ONLY CHOICE I HAVE MAKES ME SICK?

Then I may be forced to look at what got me into my current situation. I may have to review all my alternatives several times. If the only choice I have leaves me ill, then I can examine the choices I have for caring for myself under those conditions.

—and—

I may discover that the sickness I encounter comes from lack of self care, mixed with a poor mental diet. I may have to rethink how to take care of myself in my current condition. I may require huge changes in diet, rest, work and activity.

❄

Illness points to needed changes if I pay attention to the clues.

❊

WHAT IF . . .

THEY NEVER GIVE ME AN ANSWER?

Then somehow I may feel that I have made an error. I may feel that others overlooked me for reasons beyond my understanding. I may be "left dangling" with no answer. I can let thoughts over this matter consume me or I can withdraw to protect my feelings.

—and—

I can take "no answer" as an answer. I can see this as a closed door. I can refuse to knock on a closed door and move onto doors that are open for me.

❊

I can act on my own behalf, even when others offer me silence on issues of importance to me.

❋

WHAT IF . . .

OTHERS GET ALONG BETTER WITH EACH OTHER THAN THEY DO WITH ME?

Then I may feel left out or assume that something is wrong with me. I may think I have a personality flaw that others are reacting to. I may withdraw or try harder to "fit in."

—and—

I can look at what the others have in common with each other and see if that is important to me. I can take myself out of the scene to look at what is going on around me to see if I even want to be there. I can approach others one-on-one and sort out the persons I wish to be with. I can ask myself if I want to fit in or if I want to look for other places where I feel I fit in better.

❋

When I find I don't fit in, I let go of assumptions that there is something wrong with me.

❀

WHAT IF . . .

I AM CHARGED WITH A CRIME?

Then I will likely feel defensive and want to be relieved of the burden of having to answer to someone else for my actions.

—and—

I can choose the way I want to get out from under this burden. I can always make choices that are in my best interest. I can examine my own actions and make a decision that serves me well. I can ask for and receive help.

❀

I always have choices that are in my best interest.

❈

WHAT IF . . .

IT SEEMS LIKE EVERYONE IS PICKING ON ME?

Then it may be time for me to examine how I am getting along with the important people in my life. I may feel overwhelmed and unloved or heavily criticized. I may feel that I can't find the right response to the people in my life.

—and—

I can decide what my role is in getting along with others. I can make a choice to ignore, confront, explain my actions or withdraw. I can wait to respond in the way I feel best represents my feelings and wishes.

❈

I can look at how I interact with others to see what changes, if any, I need to make. I can respond in a way that serves me well.

❀

WHAT IF . . .

I COULD NOT STOP WORRYING?

Then I could look at how worrying fills my time and what I could be doing instead. I could let what I worry about guide me to the right action in my situation. I could list ways out of my situation that come to me as I worry.

—and—

If I worry a lot, I may have to let myself get tired of doing it. I may learn the affects of too much worry on me. I can also look at what helps me to finally stop worrying; whatever it is may be the clue to get my worrying under control.

❀

*I can study the way I let go of worry to
help me reduce my worries on
a regular basis.*

❈

WHAT IF . . .

MY PARTNER AND I DISAGREE ON JUST ABOUT EVERYTHING?

Then I will feel troubled by most of our interactions. I may fear speaking up for myself and my concerns. I may hide my real views so that we can have some peace.

—and—

I can look at the source of our arguments and find what is causing the conflicts. I can look at the effects on each of us. I can ask that we set aside all other commitments to look at what is important to us. I can make sure I know what is important to me. I can choose to offer my opinions and ideas in a way they can be heard.

❈

I can examine the role of conflict in my interaction with my partner. I can approach my partner in a new way so that I can be heard.

———— ❁ ————

WHAT IF . . .

I CAN'T STOP TALKING ABOUT MY PROBLEM?

Then I may have to deal with others' reactions to my need to talk so much. I may feel overwhelmed and not know what to do with my feelings.

—and—

I may find talking helps get the problem to a manageable level. I can make sure I am listening to what I'm saying so that I can hear possible solutions if they come up. I can trust my urge to talk as a needed step to reach a level of resolution. I can find persons who are willing to listen.

❁

I can use all the talking I'm doing to help me figure out my next step.

—❀—

WHAT IF . . .

GOD DOESN'T ANSWER MY PRAYERS IN THE WAY I REALLY WANT?

Then I will feel puzzled, perhaps bitter and probably let down or discouraged. I may grow angry, thinking my needs have been forgotten. I may let my faith or spirituality fade away.

—and—

I now have the chance to see what the outcome will be if I work with the answer I did receive. I can ask myself if there's any reason why this answer makes sense. I may decide that there is some value in accepting the answer that came. I can choose to use my faith to explore the situation I now have.

❀

I can choose to look at the answers to my prayers through the eyes of the faith I now have.

❦

WHAT IF . . .

I ALLOW MYSELF TO CRY WHEN I FEEL THE NEED?

Then I may feel awkward at first and tell myself I have no right to my feelings. I may wonder what others think of me if I cry in public. I may feel I need to apologize to those I am with.

—and—

I can choose to realize that my tears can help me when I release them. I can release tension when I cry. I can start thinking clearly again if I let my tears cleanse me. I can find the power to make good decisions for myself when I have released my tears.

❦

My tears are healers; they have the power to cleanse and renew me.

JUNE

i am hungry
for my power
not to control
but to remember
who i am
who i came here to be
and what i am to do.

i am hungry
for faith in me
that moves me to action

i am hungry to
feed on my birthright

I can feed
on faith in myself
one act after another

I face my fear
apply my faith
I walk one step
and then another

WHAT IF . . .

I WAS SUCCESSFUL IN BUSINESS?

Then I might be surprised at what I can do. I would also feel that I had to continue to be successful for as long as I could. I would feel new pressures and have new concerns.

—and—

I would find a great opportunity to learn more about the work I have chosen to do through my success. At the same time I could learn more about myself. I might have to set limits on what I ask myself to do for the business and check these often to see if they work. This could be a great adventure with hard work and personal growth rolled into one.

My own work can teach me a lot about my own needs and caring for myself.

❀

WHAT IF . . .

I FALL IN LOVE WITH THE WRONG PERSON?

Then I am likely to feel some discomfort from the beginning. I may feel attracted and frightened at the same time. I may also hear from others that this person is not right for me. Or I may get a growing sense that I don't belong with this person.

—and—

I may try to make it work with this person anyway. I may discover that being alone is very difficult for me. I may may learn that I will fill my time with anything to avoid being alone. If I try to squeeze myself into a frame that this person wants me to fill, I can slowly recognize this frame doesn't fit me. A mismatch may result. I can take the steps I need to take to deal with the mismatch and honor my own needs.

❀

If I am mismatched in a relationship, I see and meet my own needs.

WHAT IF . . .

I EXAMINED MY THOUGHTS?

Then I might discover some things that need changing. I might be really shocked at the contents of my thoughts. I might also find that my thoughts affect what goes on in the world around me even if I don't say them.

—and—

I might come to see that I can change my thoughts more easily than I thought. If I choose to see that I can change my thoughts, then I can also see the responsibility I have, at least in part, for the moods and attitudes I have.

I can change my thoughts and see the difference in my moods and attitudes.

❦

WHAT IF . . .

I CAN'T SPEAK THE LANGUAGE?

Then I will know a unique kind of loneliness that others have felt when they go to a new place. I will be forced to listen more carefully and become more observant of the actions of those around me. I may become a student again in order to understand.

—and—

I may learn real value in listening to the meaning of communication through sounds and by reading people's gestures. I may also learn that some things, such as a smile, are the same in any language. I may learn some of the universal aspects of any language. As I become a student again, I learn in a new exciting way.

❦

I become a student again when I am in new place.

❊

WHAT IF . . .

I FEEL TRAPPED IN MY RELATIONSHIP?

Then this lets me know I need to look closely at it and figure out what is giving me this feeling. I can examine my relationship to see what is hindering me and what is making me feel trapped.

—and—

I need to honor this feeling of being trapped. There is something to learn from it. It may be that my loved one feels closer than anyone ever has; it may be that there is a mismatch between me and my partner. I need to figure out what part of me feels trapped and find out what is needed to free myself from this feeling.

❊

Feeling trapped is a feeling I must honor whenever it happens. I can look at it and discover what I need to do to free that part of me.

❀

WHAT IF . . .

I MOVED THE BARRIERS BETWEEN ME AND OTHERS?

Then I might be taking on too much. I might let myself feel responsible for others' feelings and how they need to take care of those feelings. I might take on the lion's share of responsibility for my relationships.

—and—

I still might not have the outcome I want. I can try to remove my part of the barriers between me and others. I can also let them do what they want to do about their part in our relationship. I can grow from doing my part and seeing what others are willing to do about their parts.

❀

I can decide what my part is in my relationships, and I can take care of it. I let others do the same.

WHAT IF . . .

I GAVE MYSELF A FAMILY OF OTHERS WHO REALLY SUPPORT ME?

Then I would give up a measure of loneliness that perhaps has been with me for a long time. I would learn to accept support and hear criticism from time to time. I would also be asked to give support as part of this family.

—and—

I would learn what it's like to give and receive support. I would learn to lean on others and let them lean on me. I would learn to deal with others seeing me as I really am. I would learn that they could accept me as I am.

❀

When I give myself a family of others who really support me, I learn a balance between giving and receiving.

❄

WHAT IF . . .

I HAVE A FEELING AND I LET MYSELF FEEL IT, AND THEN I LET IT GO?

Then I can see that feelings are not permanent. I can see that I have some say in what I am feeling at any given moment. Or I can choose to stay with that feeling by seeing it as permanent while allowing myself to be a victim. I can let my feelings swallow me up or feel drowned by them.

—and—

I can choose to do what I want with the feelings I have. I can stay with them as long as I need to, and I can let them go. Feeling them and letting them go when I am done feeling them means I am human and normal.

❄

What I do with my feelings is up to me. Staying with a feeling and letting it go are both normal.

❀

WHAT IF . . .

MY SPOUSE/EX-SPOUSE HATES OUR CHILD?

Then I will feel pressure to make up for what my child is missing. I may try to be two parents and go past my own limits. I may feel pity for my child and try to protect him/her from all pain.

—and—

I could talk to myself about what is reasonable for me to do. I can choose to get professional help for myself and my child if I see the need. I can choose to hold a strong positive image of my child in my mind. And I can let my child deal with and learn from this situation since he/she may be forced to face it.

❀

I can work with myself and my child in ways that get us through the worst of life's situations.

❀

WHAT IF . . .

I HAD ALL I NEEDED WHEN I WAS A CHILD?

Then what would be different for me today? I could let go of bitterness and resentment for what I did not have or I could learn new ways of finding what I need today. If I had all I needed as a child, I would probably be in a very different place than I am today.

—and—

I would discover that I have different gifts to offer myself and others because of it. I would not be the person I am today. I would know other things and be able to do other things than I can today. What I have done with events of my life are gifts I give to myself.

❀

Having all I needed as a child would have prepared me differently for today. I would bring different gifts to the circle of life.

❃

WHAT IF . . .

A FRIEND'S BEHAVIOR THREATENS WHAT I WANT TO DO?

Then I will have to take a close look at my own priorities. I will have to reexamine my loyalties and the boundaries I have between me and my friend. I may feel very scared.

—and—

I may want to give up what is important to me to continue the relationship or to smooth out conflict. I can grow from this threatening situation. I can reaffirm the importance of my own boundaries and decide who deserves my loyalties.

❃

I make choices about my boundaries and loyalties that honor me.

❀

WHAT IF . . .

I CAN'T GET THE INFORMATION I NEED TO SOLVE MY PROBLEM?

Then I may feel frustrated and even stupid. I may blame myself as a way of handling the fact that the information is not available to me. I may also complain bitterly about not being able to get the information.

—and—

In doing this I give up on trying to get the information I need. Complaining may take the place of trying new ways to search for what I need. I can try new ways to find the information or learn new skills that can help me access what I need. I can also ask for help and receive it.

❀

When I need information, I can look at the ways I am trying to get it. I am willing to learn new ways.

WHAT IF . . .

MY PARENTS CUT ME OFF?

Then I will most likely feel hurt and angry. I may even want to contest their decision. I may want revenge or I may want to complain to my siblings about their decision. I may tell myself how unfair my parents are and see myself as a victim.

—and—

I can also decide what I have done that may have prompted this decision. I can ask myself if I took a stand with my parents that was very important to me and very unimportant to them. I can reexamine the principle behind my decision and see if I need to continue to support it. I can learn how to support myself in all ways so that parental support means less to me and my own ways mean more.

❀

I can choose to depend on myself for the support I need.

❈

WHAT IF . . .

I CAN NEVER FIND ANYONE TO LIVE WITH ME AGAIN?

Then I may feel a lot of sadness, even self-pity. I can face this idea and ask myself where it came from. Did it come from someone else? Do I actually believe this to be true of me?

—and—

I can look at what I need to change in myself if I plan to live with someone else again. I can take this time alone to learn to be comfortable with myself. I can learn to live with myself and become comfortable being alone. I can seek company in my own time and on my own terms.

❈

I can choose my reaction to the thought that I will always be alone. I can use time alone to know myself well.

❀

WHAT IF . . .

I LOSE EVERYTHING I HAVE WORKED FOR ALL THESE YEARS?

Then I am going to feel like something or someone has died. All that I have known about myself in relation to the world around me will change. I will have a new relationship to the world around me.

—and—

This may feel really strange. I may have to rely on the goodwill of others at first and receive help. I may see only my basic needs at first and learn new ways to meet these needs. I may let myself be comforted by tiny things—things I never had the time to notice before.

❀

In losing all I have, I may gain a vital understanding of what is really important in life.

❀

WHAT IF . . .

I LET MYSELF FEEL JOY AND IT NO LONGER SCARES ME?

Then I will have to let go of the feeling of fear and see what comes in its place. I will learn that feelings come and go and that none of them are permanent. I may have to deal with desire to hold on to the joy and let go of the fear.

—and—

Feeling joy without fear is part of healing from old wounds. I can let myself do this as it begins to feel comfortable. I can hold on to the fear that I feel with the joy as long as I need to; then I can let go of it when the time is right. I can see both feelings as normal.

❀

The fear I felt with joy was a necessary caution in my past. I can let it go when the time is right.

❈

WHAT IF . . .

THERE ARE NO ALTERNATIVES TO MY PROBLEM?

Then I am likely to feel a sense of hopelessness and helplessness. I may feel trapped. I may feel like I am being treated unfairly by a power greater than me.

—and—

I may refuse these feelings to continue my search for alternatives. Or I may look for some meaning that I have missed in my current situation. I may also look at what is helping me to cope.

❈

When I see no alternatives to my situation I still have many choices in how to respond.

❀

WHAT IF . . .

MY FAMILY BLAMES ME FOR THE FAMILY'S PROBLEMS?

Then I may feel I am the scapegoat. I may feel that this is unfair, and I may feel very angry at the others in my family. I may want to blame others, withdraw from them or fight with them.

—and—

I have many choices on how I can respond. I can look at my role in the family problems. I can look at changing what I think needs to be changed about myself. I can determine my parts in the family problems and work on them. I can ask for help from outsiders or professional counselors. I can define myself the way that best suits me.

❀

I define myself the way I want and refuse others' definitions of me.

=❀=

WHAT IF . . .

I HAVE TO TAKE CARE OF MY PARENTS IN THEIR OLD AGE?

Then I may feel pulled between the responsibilities I have with the family I created and the family I came from. I may feel "sandwiched" between these two groups. I may feel stretched beyond my limits.

—and—

If I can see this coming, then I can plan reasonable alternatives with my parents and siblings or services in our community. I can learn the options open for the care of my parents and help them to understand these options ahead of the time they will need them. I can ask for help from others and allow them to help me stay within the limits of my energy.

❀

I prepare for the care of my parents as they age without taking on all the responsibility myself.

❀

WHAT IF . . .

THE PEOPLE I RESPECT THE MOST DON'T LIKE WHAT I DO?

Then I may feel a lower sense of my own worth when I am around them. I may yield to their decision-making ability and give up on my own ability.

—and—

I may learn what is precious to me. I may learn to look inside myself for answers instead of to others. I may learn to rely more on what I think than on what others think, including highly-respected others.

❀

In the presence of highly-respected people, I still look within myself for answers.

❃

WHAT IF . . .

I HAVE TO WAIT LONGER THAN I PLANNED TO REACH MY GOAL?

Then I am likely to feel impatient and a sense of "it will never get here." I may want to rush through all the steps to get to my goal.

—*and*—

In rushing I may miss the "forests and the trees." As I wait longer than I want for my goal, I can take the the extra time to study aspects related to my goal in some depth. I can make good use of the extra time. I can explore issues that will add to the final goal. I can tell myself "one day at a time."

❃

I will arrive at my final goal at the right time for me. Delays in reaching my goals offer me chances to learn other things.

❧

WHAT IF . . .

MY CHILDREN DON'T THINK I LOVE THEM ENOUGH?

Then I may feel that I have to try much harder. In trying harder, I may exhaust myself and become very emotionally upset. I can listen to the needs and wishes of my children.

—and—

I can use the needs and wishes of my children as cues for me as a parent. Cues do not mean that I must do what they say. Cues from my children help me think about their real needs—spoken and unspoken. I can look at my own role in meeting these needs and determine what is reasonable for me. I can get help from professionals if I see the need for it.

❧

I take cues from my children about what they need.

❧

WHAT IF . . .

I HAVE GOOD FRIENDSHIPS
THAT WORK?

Then I have many precious gifts that need tender care. I will see a responsibility I have to nurture these relationships. I come to understand the need to give and receive.

—and—

I have the chance to see the depth of human caring and empathy. These may be new feelings and experiences for me. I may grow to a new understanding of my own purpose and the purposes of loved ones in my life as a result of having these friendships.

❧

***My good friendships are precious gifts
that need nurturing and tender
care from me.***

❁

WHAT IF . . .

I AM EARLY AND NO ONE IS THERE?

Then I may tell myself that I am there on the wrong day or at the wrong time or that no one wanted to meet me there. If I am early, I may find that I have some unexpected free time on my hands.

—and—

I can refuse to judge myself regardless of the outcome of this experience. I can choose to use the extra time to relax, meditate, plan my day or just take in my surroundings. I can notice tiny things that give me joy—things that I ordinarily would overlook.

❁

If I am early or late, I can use the time to increase my sense of well-being.

WHAT IF . . .

I DON'T FIT IN WITH ANYONE I KNOW?

Then I may feel very uncomfortable, especially if I know the people I am around. I may tell myself to work harder to fit in or that there is something wrong with me because I don't feel that I fit in with the others.

—and—

I may choose to see that this is a good time to appreciate the differences between me and others. I can choose to see myself and others as unique expressions of a Higher Power's creativity. I can choose to appreciate my unique qualities and stand behind my differences.

❀

I see uniqueness in all people and in every situation I support my own uniqueness.

❀

WHAT IF . . .

I GO TO JAIL?

Then I may be faced with feelings of resentment, bitterness, and anger. I may feel that I am being treated unfairly. I may also feel out of control.

—and—

I still have choices to make in how I respond to any situation I am faced with. I can think about what brought me to this point and what can be learned from it. I can let myself feel all the feelings I have for as long as I need, and then I can do something different than before.

❀

No matter what situation I find myself in, I still have choices in how I will respond.

❀

WHAT IF . . .

THEY EXPECT TOO MUCH FROM ME?

Then I may discover this slowly. I may find that I have let others dictate how I am going to respond. I may find that I do entirely too much in any group effort, and I have led others to believe they can count on that from me.

—and—

I may discover that I am suffering because I do too much. This may be shocking to me. I can change my own behavior and refuse to blame my suffering on others' expectations of me.

❀

I am always in charge of how much I do.

❀

WHAT IF . . .

I LIGHTENED UP AND LOOKED FOR HUMOR IN MY WORLD?

Then I may feel that many things would go undone and I would be responsible for them being undone. I may cling to the feeling that the world is a serious place requiring serious answers from me.

—and—

I may miss the medicine that comes from humor and laughter. I may have to give up some tension and learn to laugh. I may have to listen more carefully and decide what is funny to me. I may have to relax enough to develop a sense of humor.

❀

My sense of humor is a great source of medicine for whatever ails me.

❀

WHAT IF . . .

I LET OTHERS KNOW HOW I FEEL WHEN I FEEL IT?

Then others may be very surprised at first. I may find they even ask me what is wrong with me these days. I may find they want what they are used to getting from me, whatever that may be.

—and—

I may have to help my loved ones get used to seeing me honor my feelings as they come up. I may have to let them see me do this often so they can get used to it. As I honor my feelings, I honor what is true for me. I have the chance to improve my physical and mental well-being.

❀

Honoring my feelings as they come up means that I interact with others in an honest way. I improve my physical and mental health.

❀

WHAT IF . . .

I RECOGNIZED MY OWN TALENTS?

Then I might be surprised at what I am able to do. I would have to address the questions of what to do with my own abilities. I would have to decide whether to ignore them or fully use them.

—and—

Then I would have to watch where my abilities would take me. I would have to look at the purpose of my life and what I am doing to fulfill it. I would feel a sense of responsibility for the actions around my talents: to ignore or cultivate them.

❀

If I choose to see myself as talented, then I am faced with what to do with my talents.

JULY

i am hungry
for my power
not to control
but to remember
who i am
who i came here to be
and what i am to do.

i am hungry
for faith in me
that moves me to action

i am hungry
to feed on
my birthright

I can feed
on faith in myself
one act after another

I face my fear
apply my faith
I walk one step
and then another

attend to today
and leave
the next step
to itself.

❀

WHAT IF . . .

THEY TELL ME TO CHANGE MY MIND ABOUT WHAT IS IMPORTANT TO ME?

Then I will feel pressured to please others as well as myself; I may actually feel stretched between the desires of others and my own wishes. If I feel they have more control of my outcomes than I do, then I may give in to them.

—and—

I may give up my own goals or wishes for a while. I can take this time to see what is really important to me. I can choose to redefine what is important and stand behind my choices. I can choose to see myself as more in charge than others of the outcomes in my life.

❀

I choose to see others' attempts to control me and my choices as illusions. I make and support my own choices.

WHAT IF . . .

I DON'T WANT TO ANSWER AS SOON AS THEY WANT ME TO ANSWER?

Then I must decide what my priorities are in this situation. I must decide who I will be loyal to first. I may feel pulled in many directions where my loyalties are concerned.

—and—

I can choose when, how and under what conditions I will answer anyone. I only need to be aware of the consequences of my own behavior. I can let my needs direct my choices of how I'll respond to anyone.

❀

I choose the right response to anyone based on my own needs.

※

WHAT IF . . .

I EXPERIENCED JOY IN USING MY TALENTS?

Then I might get really comfortable with being happy with my work. I might feel thrilled with my ability for the first time in my life. I might begin to have a new attitude about life in general. I would likely have to deal with the reactions of others who have not experienced joy in using their talents or may not have even discovered them yet.

—and—

I might find that my life would represent a wake-up call for others to look within themselves to identify and use their talents. I might find that others would look to me for "how to do it" answers. I could help by suggesting that they also look within themselves to discover their own talents.

※

As I enjoy the talents I have been given, others may see their chance to enjoy their own.

❋

WHAT IF . . .

OTHERS DO BETTER THAN ME?

Then I will have to think about what it means to me to do less than the best. I will have to note what I tell myself when I am not the best at something. I can accept what it means not to succeed at everything I try.

—and—

I have the chance to let others shine and appreciate their unique qualities. I can choose to see that others have their abilities and that they deserve recognition. I can remind myself of my own capabilities and enjoy the fact that others have theirs.

❋

I can see and appreciate the different abilities of myself and others.

❦

WHAT IF . . .

I DON'T KNOW HOW TO START A CONVERSATION WITH OTHERS?

Then I may feel really uncomfortable in a new place or in a crowd. I may feel awkward and desire others to do my part in conversation. I may withdraw if they do not help me out.

—*and*—

I have the chance to learn a new way of being with others by just listening at first. I can listen to how others begin to talk with each other. I can use these ways to start and choose conversations that fit me. I can also look at the few times that I have started conversations successfully and remember what I did to make them happen.

❦

In a new or strange situation, I can begin conversations more easily by using what worked for me before or by listening to others.

❀

WHAT IF . . .

THERE IS NOT ENOUGH HELP TO COMPLETE THE JOB?

Then I may feel I have to do it all myself. I may end up feeling resentment, bitterness or anger toward myself or others.

—*and*—

I can choose to do what I can and let the rest go. I can refuse to take on all the responsibility and let others share it. I can own what is mine and set reasonable limits on what I ask myself to do. I can ask for additional help and accept the response given to my request.

❀

I can choose to do what I can and let others be responsible for their parts of the job.

❁

WHAT IF . . .

SOMEONE BREAKS INTO MY HOUSE?

Then my loved ones or I may be frightened or hurt. I may feel responsible for the break-in and also feel helpless to prevent another one. I may see the reactions of loved ones and feel overwhelmed.

—and—

I have the chance to look at what it will take to help me and my loved ones feel secure. I may rearrange my priorities in terms of my work hours or purchases to secure our home. I may also consider moving or other ways for the family to feel safe again.

❁

When my loved ones or I feel threatened, I can make new boundaries.

❀

WHAT IF . . .

THERE IS NOT ENOUGH OF WHAT I NEED?

Then I may feel I am being treated unfairly. I may resent others who have what I think I need. I may develop an envy or jealousy of them.

—and—

I can choose to look for what I need and imagine other ways to help me get what I need. I can refuse to give up trying to get what I need. I can also figure out ways to cope while I am without what I need. Either way, I can grow in my ability to cope.

❀

I can refuse to give up on what I think I need. I can learn valuable ways of coping while I am waiting to get what I need.

WHAT IF . . .

MY CHILD QUITS SPEAKING TO ME?

Then I may have to decide if I really want to know what is wrong between us. I may have to decide if I want to know my part in the problem. I may have to find some courage in myself to look at my part in our relationship.

—and—

I can spend time looking into my part and understanding my child's point of view. I can decide what to do once I have an idea about my part in the problem. I can reexamine what I expect from my children to see what's reasonable at this time.

❁

I can own my part in any problem with my child and set reasonable expectations for our relationship.

❦

WHAT IF . . .

MY PARTNER'S BEHAVIOR THREATENS WHAT I WANT TO DO?

Then I need to look at my boundaries with this person. I may need to ask myself where my loyalties lie and where they need to be at this time.

—and—

I need to look at just how threatening my partner's behavior is to me and my well-being. I may be able to get help by discussing this with a trusted person or a professional counselor. I can choose at any time to rearrange my responses so that my needs are taken care of. I recognize that I am the one who must take care of myself.

❦

I must be the one to take care of myself and let others take care of themselves as well.

❦

WHAT IF . . .

THERE WAS A WAY TO LOVE MYSELF MORE?

Then I might have to give up old ways of thinking and behaving. I might have to say goodbye to those old habits and ways of thinking about myself.

—and—

If I loved myself more, what would be better for me? What in my life would improve? Would I be more relaxed, have more free time, be more peaceful or find new interests? Loving myself more may mean less time on others' projects and more time appreciating who I am and what I like to do.

❦

Loving myself more means changes in many areas of my life.

❀

WHAT IF . . .

I HAVE TO LEAVE MY AREA?

Then I will feel the stress that goes along with moving anywhere. I will feel the burdens of getting to know a new place and losing the well-known connections of the old place. I will reconnect in a new way to the new place.

—and—

I have the chance to make some changes in the way I connect with others. I can start fresh with new people in my life and interact in new ways that are more pleasing to me. I can also take what I've learned from others to keep in touch with loved ones.

❀

Moving is a time of change and stress;
the stress feels both good and bad.
I accept both.

WHAT IF . . .

I COULD SHARE AND ENJOY OTHERS' USE OF THEIR TALENTS?

Then I would know that enjoying others' talents does not diminish my own. I would have to let go of jealousy and envy.

—and—

I could choose pride in my own abilities and give lots of time and attention to these. I would take my own talents and abilities very seriously.

❊

I can enjoy others' talents and abilities when I know and enjoy my own.

❦

WHAT IF . . .

I WAITED TILL THE LAST MINUTE TO DO THE REALLY IMPORTANT THINGS?

Then I may be faced with tension and anxiety that goes along with the last minute before important events. I may feel that others are pressuring me to do things their way. I may also feel very nervous with the demands of others and the demands on my time. Conflict may result.

—and—

I may decide that the last minute is the best way for me. I may decide that the pressure is what I need to get important tasks done. I may also decide to try a different way to see if it is better for me. The choice and the consequences are both mine.

❦

The timing of how I do things is up to me.

❀

WHAT IF . . .

I CAN'T FIND ANYONE TO
AGREE WITH ME?

Then I can take the time to reevaluate whether it is necessary to have someone agree with me. I can ask myself why this is important to me. I can also decide that I am the only one who needs to agree on the issue at hand.

—and—

I can decide the role of others' approval in this situation and in my life as a whole. I may need to look at how I can place more value on my own approval and find a different place for the approval of others in my life. I may try to find a balance between the two.

❀

I can examine and rearrange the role of self-approval and the approval of others in my life.

❀

WHAT IF . . .

I CHANGED AND MY FRIENDS COULDN'T ACCEPT IT?

Then I may lose some friends and feel some sadness over the loss. I may try to change to keep some of my friends or I may walk away from them.

—and—

I may learn about the traits I want in a friend. I may be more careful or slower in making new friends. I may find I have a better appreciation for the friends who acknowledged the change in me and supported it.

❀

I can recognize what I need in a friend as I watch them respond to changes in me.

❧

WHAT IF . . .

OTHERS CAN'T KEEP MY SECRETS?

Then I may be learning a difficult and valuable lesson about trust. I may find much discomfort with what I told others about me. I may also find it difficult to trust again.

—and—

I may come to a new understanding of secrets, who can keep them and who cannot. I may also recognize an important trait to me in a friend.

❧

I learn to trust from trying to trust.

WHAT IF . . .

I FEEL THAT I NEVER HAD PARENTS?

Then I may feel unloved and nervous in all new situations. I may find it hard to trust others. I may also feel that I am unlovable deep down inside.

—and—

As an adult I have the chance to challenge all of this. I can learn to be my own parent, and I can try to love myself. I can challenge the idea that I am unlovable, and I can learn to love. I can decide I will learn to trust.

❀

I refuse to be limited by negative thoughts about my parents. Each day I can learn a new way to be a loving parent to myself.

❦

WHAT IF . . .

I REQUIRED OTHERS TO PAY ME WHAT I AM WORTH?

Then I would have to stand up for my worth in each situation that I am in. I would have to recognize my own value, the value of what I do and be willing to state it to others.

—and—

I would have to be willing to deal with others' reactions to me as I state my worth. I would have to be willing to stand behind my statement of worth and explain it to others.

❦

I can choose to value myself in any situation and support this with a useful explanation.

❀

What if . . .

I EXPECT TOO MUCH FROM MYSELF?

Then I am likely to feel very disappointed when I do not meet these expectations. I am likely to think so highly of what I should be able to do that I won't recognize that my expectations are out of range.

—and—

I can learn from these disappointments. I can see when I am disappointed over and over that I need to set realistic limits for myself. I can also see the need to be kinder and gentler with myself.

❀

Setting limits for myself does not trap me; limits respect my energy level.

❀

WHAT IF . . .

I HAVE TO ANSWER FOR SOMEONE ELSE'S BEHAVIOR?

Then I have to decide how much responsibility is in fact mine. I may feel outside pressure to take on more than what is mine.

—and—

I can take this time to figure out my role in a situation that I share with another person. I can own my own role and state what I think the other person's role is as well. I only need to answer for my share of the influence in this situation.

❀

I can determine my role in any situation where I have influence and answer for that role.

❀

WHAT IF . . .

I FELT SEXUALLY INADEQUATE?

Then I might feel that I am the only one with this problem or that it's too private to discuss with someone else. I might also think that something is wrong with my body.

—and—

I might consider the sources of where I learned about my body and sexual responses. Where did I learn about sex? What was I told about my body? What do I believe about it now? What can I do about what I need to know now? What do I specifically need to change now?

❀

I can look at what I know about sexuality today and grow more comfortable with it over time.

❧

WHAT IF . . .

I BECAME READY TO WORK ON MY HOPES AND DREAMS?

Then I could plunge ahead and begin to work. I might feel scared with each new step, fearing that my hopes and dreams might leave me looking foolish.

—and—

I could call up the courage I have to begin and to continue. I could decide to have faith in myself and ask my Higher Power to assist me in the process. I would learn the meaning of taking one moment at a time.

❧

I work on my hopes and dreams one moment at a time.

❀

WHAT IF . . .

MY CHILDREN EXPECT ME TO DO EVERYTHING FOR THEM?

Then somewhere along the way I have contributed to this idea. I may end up exhausted or in poor health if I choose to do everything for my children.

—and—

Whatever they need to learn in life may be learned through my eyes instead of their own. I can examine my role in their need for me to do everything for them. I can change what I need to change so they can learn what is needed in ways that make sense to them.

❀

I can look at the role I take with my children and decide how much help I need to offer.

❀

WHAT IF . . .

I GAVE UP MY NEED TO CHANGE EVERYTHING?

Then simultaneously I would be giving up my need to control everything around me. I might be very lonely without my attention to getting my own way and controlling the events in my life. Suddenly I would have lots of time on my hands.

—and—

I might have to make choices on how to use the extra time I have now. I might have to develop some new interests. I might have to get used to more calm moments and let others do their own things.

❀

***Giving up the need to change
everything will free me.***

❀

WHAT IF . . .

I HAD MUCH MORE FUN?

Then I would have to give up being so serious and quit seeing only the serious side of things in my life. I would have to forfeit old meanings I have for new ones. I would have to enjoy some new things and have the courage to try some new things.

—and—

If I had more fun, would my attitudes change? Would I notice a change in my health and in the way I interact with others? Is there a way to find fun in all I do?

❀

I can look for fun and find it in all I do.

WHAT IF . . .

I TRUST TOO MUCH AND THEN PAY FOR IT LATER?

Then I will feel disappointed, let down and hurt. I may feel angry and vengeful. I can assess the ways that I have come to trust and reassess these values.

—and—

I can see if I trust too quickly, possibly from a long ignored emotional need. I can ask myself if I expect others to offer the trust I should give to myself. I can look at the times when trust worked well for me to determine how to begin trusting again.

❀

I assess the ways I trust to determine what has worked for me. I try these ways and discard the ones that do not work.

WHAT IF . . .

MY PARTNER HAS A PROBLEM S/HE CAN'T SOLVE?

Then I may have to step back and watch him/her try to cope with it. I may find this hard to watch, especially if I think I can solve it. I may have to let my partner ask for help and learn to receive it.

—and—

I can let my partner solve his/her problem at his/her own pace. I can refuse to jump in and solve his/her dilemma. I can offer help or wait to be asked for it. I can set limits on my helpfulness.

❀

I can figure out the best way to help my partner. I can stand back when I need to let my partner learn.

❀

WHAT IF . . .

I FIND THAT I'D RATHER
BE SOMEONE ELSE?

Then I am going to be disappointed for as long as I wish this. I can impersonate the other person and I will find that I am still me. Even if I convince myself that I am that person, I will still have the limitations that belong to me.

—and—

I can learn about the traits of the person I long to be and add these to who I am. My longing to be someone else is a real clue that I need to work on loving and appreciating myself. Longing to be anyone but myself leads me away from the precious gift I have in myself.

❀

If I long to be anyone, it is the fullest
person I can be.

❋

WHAT IF . . .

THERE AREN'T ENOUGH RESOURCES TO GO AROUND?

Then I will be required to think about how the current resources are being used. I may have to look at how the resources are being generated and come up with some new ways to generate more.

—and—

I may have to rethink how resources can best be used and by whom. I may have to design a way to use fewer resources and find ways to conserve what is on hand. In all of this, I can choose to examine my own decisions and the impact these have on available resources.

❋

Choosing to look at my own use of resources is the beginning of conservation and responsible use.

WHAT IF . . .

I NEED TO STAND UP TO MY PARENTS AND I AM AFRAID TO DO THIS?

Then I may feel angry deep within myself if I don't take the opportunity to stand up to my parents. I must also honor the fear inside me. I must see it as real for another point in time. The anger might feel bigger than me.

—and—

I can choose to see myself as big enough to handle this fear now. I have little chance of clearing the air with them when I do not honor my own feelings. I will continue to struggle where my parents are concerned if they do not know my real feelings. It will give me the chance to see when I need to stand up to others.

❊

I can clear the air when I honor my own feelings.

AUGUST

i am hungry
for my power
not to control
but to remember
who i am
who i came here to be
and what i came to do.

i am hungry
for faith in me
that moves me to action

i am hungry
to feed on my birthright

I can feed on faith in myself
one act after another

I face my fear
apply my faith
I walk one step
and then another

attend to this day
leave the next step
to itself

Faith is MY POWER
one step at a time

WHAT IF . . .

I DON'T HAVE ENOUGH MONEY FOR GROCERIES?

Then I will need to think about the money coming in and when I'll receive it. I'll need to think about how I am spending the money I have. I can also make a list of ways to get out of my current situation and decide which one is the most reasonable.

—and—

For now I can look at ways to stretch what I have left and ways to bring in more money for the food I need. Maybe I can provide a service in trade for what I need. My response is still my choice.

❧

In rough times I can still figure out a way to meet my needs.

※

WHAT IF . . .

I GET AN ULCER FROM WORRYING?

Then I may have to rethink how I live and what things I spend my time on. I may have to rethink how often I give in to concern; I may have to find a substitute for it. I may have to be willing to give up my continual fretting.

—and—

I may find a replacement in the practice of faith in a Higher Power, in myself or in both. I may have to substitute thoughts and speech full of worry with those full of faith.

※

I can choose faith over worry.

❈

WHAT IF . . .

I CAN'T MAKE MY CAR PAYMENTS?

Then I may feel ashamed or embarrassed or both. I may fear the reaction of the loan company or bank officials. I may let this affect my health and attitude every day.

—and—

I have choices. I can look at what can be done to keep making the payments. I can look at other options: selling the car, letting the bank repossess it or filing bankruptcy. I can choose to see that my life is not out of control as long as I make reasoned choices on my behalf. I may discover ways of solving the problem that I had not thought of before, simply by asking questions and looking at my options. I can still choose to support my highest good.

❈

I choose actions which support my highest good even in rough times.

❦

WHAT IF . . .

I DON'T CATCH ON QUICKLY ENOUGH?

Then I may think that I am slow or inadequate or even stupid. I may resent others who do catch on quickly. I may convince myself that I should withdraw.

—and—

I can accept that I warm up slowly to some things. I can allow myself all the time I need. I can tell myself that I will know enough about what I am learning when I need to know it.

❦

***I catch on at the pace and time
that is right for me.***

WHAT IF . . .

I BELIEVED ALL PEOPLE MADE A CONTRIBUTION TO THE PLANET?

Then I would let go of envy and jealousy. I would be less likely to compare myself to others. I would give up on waiting for someone to discover me.

—and—

I would discover my abilities and talents myself. I would enter into an agreement with myself to know and develop my abilities and talents. I would respect my own talents and have room in my life to respect the talents of others.

❀

*I am enhanced by the talents
I choose to use.*

❧

WHAT IF . . .

I SAID APPROVING WORDS ABOUT MY BODY?

Then I would have to give up comparing my body parts to those I see on TV and in magazines. I would have to stop hating imperfection in myself. I would give in to imperfection and see it more as unique difference.

—and—

I would have to stop sending hate messages to the areas of my body that are not perfect. In their place I would send messages of love and approval, and my body could begin to accept these as fitting. I would see my body make its own adjustments as it would become warmed by loving messages.

❧

I send loving messages to the imperfect parts of my body.

❃

WHAT IF . . .

I HAD TO LIVE WITH VERY FEW THINGS?

Then I would give up the need to accumulate many things. I would not have the responsibility of taking care of many things, moving them or worrying about them.

—and—

I would experience more freedom of movement. I would experience fewer attachments to things and realize what is very important to my existence on the planet. I would know only what is necessary to survive and the value of nonmaterial things.

❃

By having few things, I learn what it takes to survive and what is important beyond material things.

❀

WHAT IF . . .

I AM RUSHED INTO A DECISION?

Then I can look at how I let others decide when I should decide. I can choose to listen to them or cancel the whole process and take my time.

—and—

If I feel pressured beyond my limits, it is up to me to say so and refuse to give in to demands. I can decide when I am ready to respond. I can decide how to respond. All deadlines can be postponed until I am ready.

❀

Being in a rush is an illusion. I can refuse to be rushed.

WHAT IF . . .

I DON'T UNDERSTAND WHAT IS HAPPENING TO ME?

Then I may feel very frightened and begin to withdraw from the situation.

—and—

I can ask trusted others or seek professional help. There is no rule that says I should understand all that happens to me. I can be helped by talking to others.

❄

When I don't understand what is happening to me, then I can ask for and receive help.

❀

WHAT IF . . .

I LOSE MY DREAMS?

Then I will feel a sense of sadness and grief. I may want to give up on everything and sink into self pity or question, "Why me?"

—and—

I can feel down for as long as I need to feel this way. I can choose to dream again by looking into whatever else interests me. I can refuse to be defined by the loss of one dream.

❀

I choose to dream and work to make my dreams real. I define myself in the way I see fit, regardless of what happens to my dream.

❀

WHAT IF . . .

MY CHILDREN BLAME ME FOR ALL THEIR PROBLEMS?

Then I may feel overwhelmed with responsibility for other people's difficulties. I may feel ashamed and obliged to make it up to them. I may feel like I am being held hostage.

—and—

I can take stock of how my actions have affected my children. I can look at where they got the idea that everything was my fault. I can get professional help to figure this out. I can examine my own behavior and make needed changes.

❀

I choose to examine and accept my influence on my children. I can make the changes I need to make.

❀

WHAT IF . . .

EVERYONE EXPECTS ME
TO EXPLAIN THIS?

Then I may feel burdened. I may feel pressured to live up to everyone's expectations. I may end up feeling responsible for others' contributions and relieve them from their responsibilities in a situation.

—and—

I am likely to feel blamed if no one likes what I did. I can make a choice to answer only for my part. I can refuse to answer for anything beyond that, even when pressured to do so. I can simply repeat my answer about my part until those around me get the message that I am responsible only for myself.

❀

I explain my part in a situation and get out of the way so that others can be responsible for themselves.

WHAT IF . . .

I BEGAN TO LOVE MY MIND?

Then I would examine what I think about my own thoughts. I would have to give up negative thoughts. I would recognize that my thinking is a marvelous way of interpreting information. I would discern how I learned this information.

—and—

I would become curious about what I could do with my mind. I would give up the urge to overlook or underestimate what I could do. I could begin to expand what I believe I'm capable of doing. I might dream new dreams, set new goals and fulfill them.

❀

Loving my mind allows me to think in new ways about myself, try new things and dream new dreams.

❀

WHAT IF . . .

I FAIL A LOT?

Then I may feel "I am the failure." I may compare myself to those who do not appear to be failing. I may come to see failure as part of my personality.

—*and*—

I can choose to see failures as steps to success. I can look for the lesson in each failure, preferring to see each as more information. I can choose to be guided by an inner sense that something more important than a series of failures is happening. I can look for the process and a theme running through it.

❀

I can look at failure as information,
important to my process of living.

❈

WHAT IF . . .

I FIND ANOTHER PARTNER JUST LIKE MY FIRST ONE?

Then I may feel disappointed, especially if my first relationship did not work out the way I wanted it to. I may be scared now that the outcome of this relationship will be the same as the first.

—and—

I can look at what I learned from being in the first relationship and apply it to the second. I can pay attention to how much I have grown since the first. I can also be grateful for the similarities and differences between the two relationships. I now have the chance to finish unfinished business from the first relationship. I can also choose to behave differently now and look for different outcomes.

❈

I can grow in my new relationship from what I have learned from previous ones.

❊

WHAT IF . . .

NO ONE LETS ME SPEAK?

Then I may have to deal with anger at others. I may also have to deal with why I need others' permission to do anything, including speak.

—and—

I can give myself permission to do what I need to do when I need to do it. I can give up waiting for it to come from others. It is unlikely that others think they need to give me permission anyway. Each time I speak up for myself, I take back my power to care for myself.

❊

I own my power when I speak up for myself.

❀

WHAT IF . . .

I CANNOT SUPPORT MYSELF?

Then I am likely to feel fear and dread. I am also likely to panic. I am likely to let these fears control me.

—and—

I can make some choices that take care of my fear and dread. I can discuss my concerns with trusted loved ones. I can examine options now and plan ahead. I can accept that I will experience changes. I may use the help of a professional person. I can replace fear and panic with some kind of faith — in a Higher Power, others or myself. I can learn to live with less and trust that a way will open for me to do this.

❀

I can replace fear and panic with faithful steps that face financial barriers.

❀

WHAT IF . . .

A GOOD FRIEND MAKES A PASS AT MY SPOUSE?

Then I will be understandably hurt, confused and angry. I may feel betrayed by one or both of them. I need to allow myself to have my feelings about this situation.

—and—

When I am able to think clearly, I can decide what is important to me. I can think how I want to address this issue and with whom. I can use "I messages" to state my feelings without blame. I can assess my friend's response and my partner's response. I can take responsibility for stating the changes that are important to me.

❀

It is important to allow myself the feelings I have, state them if I choose, and make changes I need in my situation.

❋

WHAT IF . . .

I AM TOO SCARED TO TRY?

Then I am likely to feel frozen in the situation. I am not likely to move ahead, feel the longing to try or the wish to succeed.

—and—

I can look at why I am too scared to try. I can discuss this with trusted people for their feedback. I can look at the benefit, if any, of staying scared and being frozen. I can also look at what it would take to get me to try. I can challenge my fear by cutting it up into very tiny steps. I can choose to focus on each tiny step.

❋

I can manage my fear by closely examining it and cutting it up into very small steps. I can turn fear into faith by taking one small step at a time.

WHAT IF . . .

I CAN'T AFFORD THE SERVICES I NEED?

Then I may be forced to wait for what I can afford or to find a substitute for the services I need. I may fret over the fact that what I need is not available to me now.

—and—

I can look for ways to cope with the situation. I can see what I am doing now that is really helping me, even if it is only a fraction of help to me. I can challenge the idea that the services available are the only things that can help me. I can think about and seek other ways to help myself such as bartering for what I need.

❊

I refuse to be limited by the widely-used ways to help my situation. I will look for other ways that no one has used yet.

❋

WHAT IF . . .

I CAN'T MAKE A LIVING DOING THE KIND OF WORK I WANT TO DO?

Then I may be faced with some initial or continual disappointment. I may be faced with decisions to find other kinds of work to support myself while I do the work I like.

—and—

I can refuse to give up what I want to do and find work that will support the desire in my heart. I may work at what I really want to do part-time, while also doing something else I'm good at to help support me in the meantime.

❋

By finding new ways to support my heart's desire, I will see a new ingenuity in me.

❀

WHAT IF . . .

I HAVE TO RETIRE EARLY?

Then I may feel a sense of uselessness and a loss of meaning. I may be depressed for a while as I find new meaning and activities in my life. I will have to look at how I see myself as I grow older, and how I look at changes in myself.

—and—

I can enter into a new understanding of life at my age. I can try new things, even if on a small scale. I can define myself in a new way. I can discover new gifts that I have that were previously unknown to me. I can also recover old talents and use them.

❀

At any point in my life, I choose to define myself as useful.

❃

WHAT IF . . .

I FEEL WEAK?

Then this is the time I can take to focus on myself and what is going on with me. I can examine the weakness I feel or ask a professional to work with me.

—and—

I can rearrange my life to take care of the weakness I feel for the short term and the long term if necessary. I can ask for and let others' help me. I can decide the quality of life that I want for myself and work to achieve it as closely as possible. I can take the time I need to get there, too.

❃

Feeling weak is a sign that I need to take better and regular care of myself.

❁

WHAT IF . . .

I LOSE MY FAITH?

Then I may feel I am living life without a compass. I may lose my sense of direction. I may think others have answers for me and I may set them up on pedestals.

—and—

I lose my faith when I am disappointed or have particular expectations that are not met. I lose my faith when I forget to trust in a Higher Power or myself. I can regain my faith as soon as I know that I have lost it. I only need to reconnect with the source of my faith, as I have done many times before. I can ask myself, "What did I do the last time I used my faith well?"

❁

I can begin to regain my faith the moment I am aware that I have lost it.

❀

WHAT IF . . .

I FEEL LEFT OUT?

Then I am likely to feel sad and bitter. I am likely to blame others who are leaving me out. I may decide that I am not worthy to belong to the group.

—and—

I can choose what I believe about my own worth. I can decide if I really want to belong to a group that excludes people like me. I can decide if my civil rights have been violated. I can choose what I want to happen and take steps toward that end. I can trust my own impression of me. I refuse to be defined by others who practice exclusion.

❀

I take a stand on my own behalf and refuse to be defined by those who exclude me.

❀

WHAT IF . . .

I LIVED JUST THE WAY
I WANTED TO LIVE?

Then I might be viewed as odd by those who do not have the courage to try this. I would have to live on faith, courage and my own wits. I would limit my reliance on others to take care of me.

—and—

I would make choices that move me toward my goals. I would achieve my goals by focusing on them daily, and each day my actions would support those goals. I would find a way to deal with others' reactions to my choice. I could settle into a peaceful bliss, whatever way I define it.

❀

Living each day the way I want to live it requires faith, courage and the use of my own wits. The benefit is peace.

247

❦

WHAT IF . . .

I LOSE A PART OF MY BODY TO DISEASE?

Then I will likely experience shock, denial and anger. I can allow myself these expected feelings. They are a natural reaction. I may feel myself move in and out of them.

—and—

I may grow to accept, even conquer what has happened to me. These are choices that I have. I can look for new meaning in my life and let my search and wounded past guide the way. I can choose a new meaning for this event. I can refuse to be limited by physical appearance.

❦

I can always find new meaning for myself, regardless of my circumstances.

❀

WHAT IF . . .

I BELIEVED I HAD ALL I NEEDED?

Then I would stop striving and my focus in life would likely be different. I would likely find new interests, maybe help others or just rest from the struggle I have had all these years. I may feel guilty about my good fortune.

—and—

I could choose to focus on things that satisfy me. I could choose to nurture myself and my loved ones and find ways to give back the blessings I have received. I could still define myself in any situation. If I refuse to struggle, I may come to know peace.

❀

If I believe I have all I need, then I am likely to live in peace and gratitude.

❀

WHAT IF . . .

I AM WRONGLY ACCUSED?

Then I will know instant anger. I can also let it tear me apart or act irrationally.

—and—

I can let the anger I feel help me identify a strategy that will help me. I can figure out the best way to represent myself and make sure my civil rights are respected. I can let my anger help define and explain my innocence.

❀

I can use anger to help me plan a useful strategy.

❀

WHAT IF . . .

I CAN'T PAY MY BILLS?

Then I may feel panic and dread. I may fear losing everything. I may see this stress show up in my physical health.

—and—

I can choose what I need to do now. I can contact those I owe money to and be up front with them. I can work out a payment plan that will suit us both. I can look into ways to make more money. Listing all the ways I can think of may help. I can get free help from counselors at consumer credit services in my community.

❀

If I choose to look at the ways to solve my money problems, I can find a way out.

251

❀

What if . . .

I HAD A GOOD TIME WHEN I EXPECTED TO HAVE A BAD TIME?

Then I would challenge what I believe about what I enjoy. I might have to give up old ideas about what gives me pleasure and whether I should have it or not. I might be more willing to try new things.

—and—

I might be willing to let more pleasure come into my life in other areas. I might be more willing to give myself pleasure and to see pleasure as a natural part of life. I might take responsibility for giving myself pleasure in any situation.

❀

***I see pleasure as a natural
part of my life.***

SEPTEMBER

❦

i am hungry
for my power
not to control but to remember
who i am, who i came here to be
and what i am to do.

i am hungry
for faith in me
that moves me to action

i am hungry
to feed on my birthright

I can feed on faith in myself
one act after another

I face my fear, apply my faith
I walk one step and then another

attend to this day and leave
the next step to itself

Faith is MY POWER
one step at a time.

Faith is believing
acting, spending
Faith is all I need

WHAT IF . . .

I HAVE TO MOVE TO FIND WORK?

Then I will know the discomfort of moving and how it feels to disconnect with what I know and reconnect with what I don't know. I will likely feel sadness mixed with many other feelings.

—and—

I can view this as a new beginning for me. I can remember how I made a home elsewhere, and how I can do those things which helped me before. I can begin again in ways that are pleasing to me. I can choose to see this move as the beginning of a new part of my life.

❃

I can choose to think about moving to a new area as the beginning of a new part of my life.

❀

WHAT IF . . .

I CAN'T DO THE WORK IN SCHOOL?

Then I am in the position of deciding whether I can ask for help. I may feel ashamed, embarrassed or awkward. I may feel I want to quit.

—*and*—

I can choose a new way for myself. I can decide that I am worthy of the best help I can get to understand the work. I can refuse to be distracted from my goal. I can allow myself to ask for and receive help.

❀

I can ask for and receive exactly the help I need.

❧

WHAT IF . . .

I GIVE UP IN THE MIDDLE OF AN IMPORTANT PROJECT?

Then I may be disappointed in myself or I may feel ashamed. I may justify why I gave up to others, while feeling I let myself down.

—and—

I can learn what it is that bothers me enough to want to quit in the middle of an important project. I can analyze whether or not it is the project itself. I can examine my feelings to determine what it is I must honor. I can then choose how I will treat this situation.

❧

When I leave a project before it is finished I take the time to understand why.

❀

WHAT IF . . .

I BELIEVED I COULD DO WHAT I WANTED TO DO?

Then I would have to stop all the thoughts I've had about not being able to do the things I want to do. I would see how often I tell myself the things I want are not possible. I would face my doubt.

—and—

I would begin several new habits. I would replace the old thoughts with new ones that encourage me to try. I would begin each new project with a joyful certainty about what is right for me to do. I would begin each day thinking about the next step in my project. I would be thankful for being able to do what I am doing.

❀

Believing I can do what I want to do involves forming new habits and feeling grateful.

257

WHAT IF . . .

MY LIFE BECAME AN ADVENTURE?

Then I might be inclined to tell myself to be more serious. I might look for distractions that help me to be with others who see life as a serious thing. I might feel the pressure of others who say "change and be like us."

—and—

Even tiny things could bring me joy—joy in the knowledge that human experience is somehow divinely inspired. I would get joy from a tiny ant, a pebble, the roaring ocean and the wilderness inside and around me. I would approach each step in my path with curiosity and care.

❃

If I let my life be an adventure, even the smallest thing brings joy.

❀

WHAT IF . . .

I HAVE AN ANXIETY ATTACK?

Then I may be embarrassed or unable to cope with my surroundings for a short period of time. I may have to rely on others for help. I may need to find the source of the anxiety.

—and—

I can learn from the moments of anxiety. I can learn what needs healing in me. I can try to understand the source of the anxiety and what I can do about it. I have the opportunity to learn to make myself feel more safe.

❀

Moments of anxiety offer me the opportunity to figure out how to make myself feel safe.

❦

WHAT IF . . .

I SPENT TOO MUCH TIME WORRYING ABOUT OTHER PEOPLE'S FEELINGS?

Then I may suddenly feel neglected. I may feel that no one cares about me and that I cannot get the help I need. I may feel pressure to take care of others' feelings before I attend to my own.

—*and*—

I may have to look at separating myself from other people's feelings. I may have to take the time to know my own feelings and put a name on them. I can also look at what benefit I get from taking on everyone else's feelings.

❦

I can look at what I do with other people's feelings and make the changes I need.

WHAT IF . . .

MY CHILDREN LOSE FAITH IN ME?

Then I will feel hurt and disappointed in myself. I may fear that they will turn away from me. I may lose hope that we can have a relationship with each other.

—and—

I have the chance to hear and see what is on their minds. I can open myself to the reasons that we have a problem between us. I can learn what they expect of me, and I can decide what is reasonable for me to expect of myself when I am with them.

❀

When I have a problem with my children, I choose to learn how they see things. I choose to share my views with them in a reasonable way.

❦

WHAT IF . . .

I GET HURT?

Then I will know pain. I will feel down—physically, mentally or emotionally—for a while. I may have to rely on help from others.

—*and*—

I have the chance to learn how to protect myself better in the future. I can understand myself, my needs and what is important to me. I can begin practicing the self-care that I need now.

❦

Getting hurt teaches me how I need to care for myself. When I am hurt I set boundaries that protect myself.

WHAT IF . . .

I CAN'T BELIEVE IN MYSELF ENOUGH?

Then I will feel a longing to be what I can be. I will long to know myself at the deepest level—to know my purpose, my place and where I fit in.

—and—

I can learn to believe in myself. I can give myself the understanding and the room to grow in self-belief. I can acknowledge where I am coming from and why my self-belief is low. I can discover habits that I already have indicating a belief in myself. I can expand on these habits to gain more confidence in myself and even more good habits. I have the chance to believe in myself more.

❀

I can learn to believe in myself. I can make this a habit.

WHAT IF . . .

I CAN'T GET EVERYTHING DONE IN ONE DAY?

Then I may feel let down or I may have to deal with someone else's disappointment in me. Or I may need to loosen and lessen my expectations of myself.

—and—

I may give up the idea that I am a super person. I have the chance to set realistic expectations of myself for one 24-hour period, including some fun and some rest. I have the chance to get a balance in what I do each day.

❃

I can find the daily balance I need in work, rest and play.

❋

WHAT IF . . .

MY FRIENDS STOP BEING MY FRIENDS BECAUSE OF MY CHOICES?

Then I am likely to feel sad and a bit angry. I may feel that I am being treated unfairly. I may want to argue my point or withdraw from them. I may feel isolated and lonely.

—and—

This is also a chance for me to see what I mean to those friends who are disappointed in my choices. I can rethink how or if I want to be with them. I can choose to rethink my choices. I can look at the traits I consider most important in a friend and see who stands by me. I can grow from seeing how others see me.

❋

When friends turn away from me,
I choose to rethink the situation and
look inward for how I can grow.

WHAT IF . . .

THERE IS A LOT OF PREJUDICE AT MY WORKPLACE?

Then I may feel the scorn of others. I may feel crowded and guarded in all I do. I may feel unsafe.

—and—

I can choose whether I will let others' ignorance and attitudes control me. I will present the person that I want them to see in me, and let how I live speak for me. I will define myself in all situations. I will do so with pride.

❀

I choose how I will define myself in all situations.

❊

WHAT IF . . .

I AM NEVER HIRED AGAIN TO DO WORK FOR OTHERS?

Then I may feel like something is wrong with me because no one wants to hire me. I can let myself believe that my usefulness is over. I can feel hopeless.

—and—

I can choose to find a new meaning for myself that includes a new way of working. I can create a new kind of job for myself by doing what I feel drawn to. I can start a new chapter in my life.

❊

I depend on my own ideas of what I should do. I let go of the need for others' approval.

WHAT IF . . .

I CHOSE TO CLEAR THE AIR EACH TIME I SAW THAT IT NEEDED TO BE DONE?

Then I may have a bit more conflict in my life at first. I may have to struggle with what is important to me and how to get others to hear it. I may see the anger in others.

—and—

I can benefit from making my feelings known when I feel them. I choose each time to protect and support my own boundaries. I can use conflict to settle my grievances and take care of my needs.

❀

I can use conflict to carve out the kind of situation that makes me comfortable.

❀

WHAT IF . . .

I AM NEVER WELL-KNOWN?

Then I can look at what is really important in my life. Do I need 15 minutes of fame? I can look at what it means to be famous and the magnetism that I feel toward it.

—and—

I can ask myself what I really need in my life. I can look over my life to see the contributions I have made to the planet and decide if I approve of them. I can put the highest value on my own approval.

❀

I can look to myself as the main source for my approval.

❀

WHAT IF . . .

I FELT I HAD SPECIAL WORK TO DO?

Then I may feel pulled between the special work and the work that others find more acceptable. If I feel I have special work to do, it may include many sacrifices I have to make. I may feel lonely.

—and—

I may realize the rewards of paying attention to what I consider as my mission or purpose. I may feel a deep sense of satisfaction and contentment. As I make my contribution, I will grow. Others will also have the chance to grow.

❀

If I do the work that I feel fits me, both others and I will benefit.

❀

WHAT IF . . .

I MAKE A REQUEST AND THEY DO NOT HONOR IT?

Then I am in the position of deciding how to handle others who do not hear my needs. I may feel very disappointed or ignored and invisible. I may feel rage.

—and—

I have the chance to be sure that my needs are heard. I can find the words to support my needs. I can choose to confront these persons and offer them a lesson that they need to remember in dealing with me. I can practice what I will say ahead of time if necessary. I can choose the best time to approach those who have forgotten me.

❀

When others ignore my requests, I am given the chance to support my needs and insist that others recognize them.

WHAT IF . . .

THERE ARE NO SUPPLIES LEFT FOR THE JOB I AM TO DO?

Then I may be confused about what to do next. Or I may feel frustrated with someone's lack of consideration or planning.

—and—

I now have the chance to come up with a creative solution. I can look to others who have the supplies for help. Or I can find alternative sources of supplies or ways to cope that have not been tried before.

❧

A lack of supplies provides a space for me to be creative with a solution.

❊

WHAT IF . . .

I BECOME A SUCCESSFUL PERSON AND DON'T KNOW HOW TO REACT TO IT?

Then I may feel awkward with the success. I may say and do things out of nervousness or anxiety that do not represent the person I really am.

—and—

I can grow into success. I do not have to know it all tonight. I can accept praise for my work, and I can acknowledge it myself. I can accept success at the pace that makes sense to me.

❊

I can grow into success
one step at a time.

❀

WHAT IF . . .

EVERYONE ENVIES ME?

Then I must look at what I have done to draw such a reaction. I may feel scared of others' reactions to my achievements. I may feel that their envy is sure to end my success. I may want to gloat, and I may want them to feel uncomfortable.

—and—

I can take this time to look over my accomplishments and appreciate them even if they surprise me. I can take a humble approach when discussing these accomplishments with others. I can take the time to discern what changes I need to work on in my relationship with others.

❀

I can see the envy of others as their problem.

❀

WHAT IF . . .

I RISKED EVERYTHING FOR MY DREAMS AND OTHERS AROUND ME WOULD NEVER DO THAT?

Then I may feel a little out of place. I may feel pressured by others to do more of what they are doing. Or I may feel that they are normal and I am crazy.

—and—

I can look now at why I have the need to compare myself to others and what they are doing. What if there are as many normals as there are people? If I continue to compare myself and what I do with what others would do, then I may miss what is normal for me.

❀

Everyone has his or her own "normalcy." We are each drawn to what is natural for us.

275

❊

WHAT IF . . .

I AM SO SCARED THAT
I WANT TO RUN?

Then I may run many times before I stop to look at why. I may experience this fear over and over until I can face it.

—and—

I can choose at any time to face the fear and find out why I need to run. I can choose to honor it and be with it until it is no longer necessary in my life. I can ask others for help or seek help from a professional counselor.

❊

***When I honor my fear and take it
seriously, I have the best
chance to change it.***

WHAT IF . . .

I CAN'T STOP THINKING ABOUT MY PROBLEM?

Then I may feel overwhelmed and controlled by it. I may feel there is no time in my life for anything else. I may panic when it gets to be too much.

—and—

I have the chance to also see what the preoccupation can provide me with. What does it keep me from doing? What do I get to do because of it? If I give it up, what will be different for me? When I am not thinking about the problem, what am I doing that might help me at other times?

❀

I can learn how to help myself by studying what I do with the preoccupations I experience.

WHAT IF . . .

I LOSE MY BEST FRIEND?

Then I will feel horrible sadness and loss. I may not be able to do much for a while. I may need to let my emotions out whenever and wherever I feel them.

—and—

I need to feel the sadness and loss. I need to let myself go through the grieving process; it is the kindest thing I can do for myself. Grieving lets me naturally respond to the pain I feel.

❀

Letting myself grieve is the kindest thing I can do for myself.

❦

WHAT IF . . .

I LOSE THE ABILITY TO THINK AND REASON?

Then I may be very frightened by anything I have to face. I may have to let others make decisions for me and I may find that I have a minimal input into those decisions. I may feel very uncomfortable with their decisions.

—and—

I can let myself think about my wishes for self-care and make those known to loved ones now. I can also choose several persons to act on my behalf and make my wishes known to them. I can let all the significant others in my life know my wishes so that it's clear to everyone who I wish to handle my affairs.

❦

I can decide my wishes now and make these known to important others.

WHAT IF . . .

THERE WERE FEWER MOMENTS IN THE DAY WHEN I FRETTED OVER WHAT TO DO?

Then I might have more free time on my hands all of a sudden. I might have to choose what to do with that time. I might find that my life is presently quite dull.

—and—

Then I could decide to flow with the rhythm of each day. I could refuse to push the river. I could release myself from so many expectations. I could discover more pleasant things to do. I could just do less. In the long run, less just might mean more.

❀

Flowing with the rhythm of each day allows me to move through my day with ease.

❀

WHAT IF . . .

I FOUND THAT I LOVED WHAT I DO?

Then I would make a commitment to do the work I love. If I loved it, then I might discover that it does not feel like work. I could move through my day with a different attitude.

—and—

I could find a creative connection with my work. I could produce that which allows me and others to grow. I could feel creative forces in my work as my love of it is an indicator of my own purpose.

❀

If I love what I do, then the creative forces can move through me.

❀

WHAT IF . . .

I HAD TO START ALL OVER AGAIN?

Then I would feel a sense of loss and frustration over where and how to begin. I may have to rely on help from others. I may choose to call on my sense of faith to help me, too.

—and—

I could do it. I could ask my faith to work through me as I move through all the feelings that come with great loss. I could choose to be very kind to myself and start over again slowly by making needed changes and keeping whatever helps me begin again.

❀

Starting over again is a difficult but "do-able" thing as long as I honor and take care of my feelings along the way.

WHAT IF . . .

I TOOK LESS TIME FOR OTHERS AND PUT MORE INTO MY OWN INTERESTS?

Then I may see some strong reactions from others who are used to having more of my time. I may have to deal with harsh disapproval from them. I may have to wait to see who will be there as a friend when the dust settles from this change.

—and—

I can look at what kind of arrangements others expected from me. I can choose to explain my new needs. I can recognize and honor the reactions of others without being driven to change.

I can make changes in how I interact with others and deal with their reactions without giving up my own needs.

OCTOBER

i am hungry
for my power
not to control but to remember
who i am, who i came here to be
and what i am to do.

i am hungry
for faith in me
that moves me to action

i am hungry
to feed on my birthright

I can feed on faith in myself
one act after another

I face my fear, apply my faith
I walk one step and then another

attend to this day and leave
the next step to itself

Faith is MY POWER
one step at a time.

Faith is believing
acting, spending
It is all I need

Faith that wrestles my fear
to the ground

❁

WHAT IF . . .

I HAVE TO DO SOMETHING I HATE TO BE ABLE TO PAY MY BILLS?

Then I may feel that life is unfair to me and only me. I may resent others who seem to be doing what they want to do and getting by in an easier way.

—and—

I can ask myself what it means to me to have work that I can do. I can look at how I cope with the job on days when I am doing well. I can look at how I make it on the days when things are rough. Keeping my eye on other options and on the fact that the bills are paid may help me to see my way through the work I do not like.

❁

***I have many ways to cope with
things I do not like.***

WHAT IF . . .

I OFFERED MYSELF TO MY IDEA OF A HIGHER POWER?

Then I would be giving up control of my life and will to something I cannot see and know only by faith. My belief may feel weak or even hypocritical.

—and—

I can see how easy and how hard it is to walk in faith. I may need to offer myself and my will to my idea of a Higher Power, especially in times of trouble. I may see this power working in the small things of my life.

❀

When I use my faith and tune in to my concept of a Higher Power, I flow with the situations of my life.

❀

WHAT IF . . .

MY LAST RESORT FAILS?

Then I will know failure. I may feel sad, disappointed and disillusioned that my plans did not work. I will be face to face with what it means to me to fail.

—and—

I can look at the options that failed and see if there were others that could have worked. I can see failure as a chance to treat this situation a whole new way or move on to doors that are open to me. I can determine what meaning I give to this situation.

❀

I can look at failure in many different ways. I choose the meaning that frees me to go on.

WHAT IF . . .

I AM LAID OFF FROM MY JOB?

Then I may be financially uncomfortable for a while. I may have to rethink expenses and buying habits. I may feel bitter with my employer and look for temporary work until I find a permanent job.

—and—

I can choose to take the break from work and decide what I need to do to keep every aspect of my life in balance. I can choose an attitude that frees my faith. I can choose to believe that I will be taken care of. I can also choose to do what I can to make my situation better and then leave the rest to my faith.

❀

During this hard time, I can choose an attitude that works for me.

❀

WHAT IF . . .

I DON'T KNOW HOW TO EXPRESS WHAT I FEEL?

Then I may feel blocked and develop habits that further block my good. I may be too scared to try to discuss how I feel.

—and—

I can decide that my first try at expressing my feelings is just that: a first try. I will improve with practice. I can get help from trusted others or a counselor. I can make a commitment to myself each time I try to express my feelings by taking care of what I feel. I can remind myself that the way I express my feelings is always up to me.

❀

The way I express my feelings is up to me. I can choose a way that takes care of me and helps others to listen.

WHAT IF . . .

I CAN'T FOCUS ON MY WORK?

Then I will be easily distracted and may fall behind. I may get very frustrated and lash out at others, even those trying to help me.

—and—

I may find that something really needs my attention and serves as a distraction at work; I may find out what that is only after much thought. If I choose to pay attention to the distraction and take care of the need now, then it is likely I will be able to focus on my work again.

❀

***When I lose my focus on work, I can
determine the cause and remedy.***

WHAT IF . . .

THE CAR WON'T START?

Then I may be late or angry or frustrated, or all of the above. I may end up financially strapped.

—and—

I may need to rethink how to improve or cope with the transportation I have. I may need to ask for information to help make this decision. I can honor whatever feelings I have. When these are dealt with, I can list and examine all the options I have.

❀

***When my transportation is lost, I can
take care of my emotions and
choose the right action.***

WHAT IF . . .

I CHANGE WHAT I THINK OF MYSELF?

Then I will feel discomfort both inside and outside of me. I may feel loss with leaving parts of me behind. And I may have to get used to new parts that are emerging in me. I also may act differently toward others and have to deal with how they react.

—and—

I now have the chance to present myself as I wish. I can support the new parts of me while letting the old parts go. I can accept that others will have their reaction to the changes in me. I can choose what I think about myself.

❋

Changing what I think about myself brings changes on the inside and the outside. I can choose how I respond to both.

❀

WHAT IF . . .

THERE IS NO ROOM FOR
ME IN THEIR PLANS?

Then I may feel left out, like I don't belong. I may also act like it doesn't bother me when it really does. I may act out my feelings without really owning them.

—and—

I can choose to look at the meaning I have given to being left out of their plans. I can ask myself if there are any other possible ways to explain what happened. I can look at the situation from the viewpoints of the other people involved to see if the meaning could be different.

❀

***In any situation I choose the meaning
of it that fits me and pleases me.***

WHAT IF . . .

MY PARTNER'S BEHAVIOR IS THREATENING MY CHILDREN?

Then I will be in the position of deciding where my loyalty lies. I may feel pulled between the relationship I have with my partner and the responsibility I have to my children. I am likely to feel caught in the middle.

—and—

I have an opportunity to take a new stand with everyone concerned. I can insist on respect for me and for anyone who is a part of my family. I can model that respect and offer consequences that make sense to family members for violation of my rules.

❧

I can insist on and model respect for those around me.

❀

WHAT IF . . .

I WOULD RATHER BE DOING SOMETHING ELSE?

Then I will let myself be easily distracted and will long for anything else to do. I may lose focus, make more errors and end up wanting to sleep or escape.

—and—

I can allow myself the feeling that I want to do something else and keep my focus at the same time. I can also choose to do something else and return later to finish the work I started. I can allow myself to change projects or remain attached to the one at hand. I can parcel out time to finish. Quitting for a break does not mean quitting forever.

❀

I know when the time is right to take a break from work.

❁

WHAT IF . . .

MY SPOUSE HAS AN AFFAIR?

Then I am likely to sense it or know it. I may feel angry, bitter, resentful or even vengeful. These are valid responses to hurt and disappointment.

—and—

I can let myself have these feelings for as long as necessary. I can be gentle to myself and let others help me when I need them. I can let my faith help me. I can choose to examine my role in our relationship and see if I want to change it. I can choose right action that honors my feelings and represents me well. I can also choose to make myself safe from further emotional injury.

❁

If I am hurt, I first honor my feelings. I make other choices that take care of me.

❦

WHAT IF . . .

RESENTMENT BECAME A THING OF MY PAST?

Then I would notice room for other things in my life—maybe other feelings, other interests, other people. I would give up expectations of others and flow with outcomes and events.

—and—

I might feel less judgmental of others and try more empathy for those I do not understand. I might experience much less disappointment. I would free myself to accept my own experiences and let others have their own.

❦

Letting go of resentment frees many parts of me.

WHAT IF . . .

I FEEL OVERWHELMED BY ALL MY PROBLEMS?

Then I will be very hesitant to try to solve any of them. I will feel as though they control me and therefore, my life may feel like it is out of control. I may withdraw and refuse to help myself.

—and—

I can decide nothing today if I want and begin to look at what I can do in a systematic manner as soon as I feel I'm ready. I can tackle each problem one at a time, asking for help if I need it. I can take on each problem at my own pace, one step at a time.

❀

Feeling overwhelmed is my cue to stop, slow down and only decide my next step.

❈

WHAT IF . . .

I LOOK DIFFERENT AS I GET OLDER?

Then I may feel a loss as I notice changes in my skin, hair and body. I may long for times when I was younger. I may resent others who are more youthful looking or who are younger.

—and—

I can choose to see what has changed in me for the better. Am I more comfortable with myself now? In what areas do I feel stronger? Do I like myself more now than when I was younger? I can view myself as losing some traits and gaining others. I can then ask myself which ones are more valuable to me.

❈

Aging is a process where I lose some traits and gain some others. I can decide on my own which I value most, and I can cultivate those in me.

299

WHAT IF . . .

I MADE DECISIONS BASED ON MY NEEDS?

Then I would have to place a high priority on what my body, heart and mind say they need. I would have to listen and recognize when I am in need.

—and—

I could decide what I need and what decisions must be made to fulfill those needs. I can hear the voices and the influence of others, but the first place I go for information is to myself. I can be alone with myself to see what is going on. I may have to ask myself, "What am I feeling right now?" and "What does this mean that I need right now?"

❦

Making decisions that meet my needs requires my constant and immediate attention.

=❀=

WHAT IF . . .

I GET TOO DEPENDENT ON OTHERS' OPINIONS?

Then I will have let my own ability to decide for myself to take a backseat to others' influence. I will be thinking more about what they think about my situation and less about my own opinion.

—and—

I may also need many others to help me because no one will be available all the time. I can challenge their opinions privately first and then think about it. I can use their information to help me decide what I want in any given situation. I can determine all my options and use my thinking ability to help me make good decisions.

❀

I choose to value my own opinion and hear the opinions of others at the same time.

OCTOBER 18

❀

WHAT IF . . .

MY PARTNER HAS A PROBLEM THAT HE/SHE DOESN'T KNOW ABOUT?

Then I am in the position of trying to decide if and how I will help. I may feel pity for my partner or I may just feel sad. I may also feel that there is nothing I can do and that it is up to my partner.

—and—

I may have to let go of my need to change things for him/her. I may have to let my partner change in his/her own way when and if he/she chooses. I may be most helpful by getting out of the way and refusing to handle this for him/her. I may have to let my partner see the consequences first and then recognize the problem.

❀

I can let my partner solve his/her own problems in his/her own way and time.

❋

WHAT IF . . .

I LOSE ALL HOPE?

Then the way I see my life may be a bleak picture; it may be very grim and sad. I may look for the negative in all my situations.

—*and*—

I may reject any glimmer of hope that comes my way. I can choose this way or I can recognize that rainy days and hopeless moments call for seed-size faith that things can change. I can choose to believe that I have such faith inside me. I need only yield to it in times that look hopeless. I can look at why I have not given up completely and grow from that.

❋

Losing all hope may be part of the cycle of my life; I can regain the hope I need by using faith the size of a tiny seed.

WHAT IF . . .

I CAN'T MAKE NEW FRIENDS?

Then I may be blocking my own way. I may need to examine what I am doing that keeps me thinking this way.

—and—

I can look at how I have made friends in the past and what I did to make it happen. I can use what worked for me before. I can think about places and activities where I am likely to find new friends. In the meantime, I can be my own best friend, being kind and gentle to myself.

❀

I can look at how I have made friends in the past and apply it to my present situation. At the same time, I can be kind and gentle to myself.

WHAT IF . . .

MY FRIENDS THINK I AM CRAZY?

Then I need to look at who has changed. I may feel insulted by them and our relationship may feel like it is dwindling away. I may feel angry and sad at the same time.

—and—

I can rethink my own behavior and talk it over with those who will listen. I can choose to hear what they have to say and try to see their points of view. I can choose to support what is going on in my life and my reactions to it by the words I choose. I can refuse to explain my behavior or justify it. I can honor my own experience and choices, without apology.

❁

I can look at any situation that involves me and take stock of my role in it.

❁

WHAT IF ...

I STUCK TO WHAT IS IMPORTANT TO ME?

Then I may see that I am alone from time to time, taking unpopular stands based on my principles. I may be laughed at or called names, or my reputation may be smeared or misrepresented. I could really suffer.

—and—

I can understand that this is to be expected with some positions that I may take. I can understand that at times I will be lonely or stand alone. I can see this as part of taking a stand. I can choose to put these reactions at the bottom of the heap of what is important to me. I can always place my principles first and feel comfort in that.

❁

I find comfort in my own principles.

WHAT IF . . .

I NO LONGER WANT TO LIVE?

Then I may be in the position to examine what has changed in my life to make me feel this way. I may need help from others, especially professionals, to help me see this.

—and—

I must honor the pain that I feel in reference to my wish to die. Wishing to die may be my longing to be in another situation. I can look at what I think would be different in that situation and see what I can do to change the current situation that's hurting me. I can get help from others. With their help, I may find what I need to change in my life.

❀

When I no longer want to live, I can honor the pain by looking at it and asking for help.

WHAT IF . . .

I SAW ALL THE EVENTS IN
MY LIFE AS LESSONS?

Then the painful meanings I give to all that happens to me would be changed. I would give up my fascination with what hurts. There would be more free time in my life.

—and—

I would focus on what I am supposed to learn in each situation that I face. I would see my life and the world around me as classes where I can learn in my own way.

❀

***Thinking about life's events as lessons
frees me to learn at my own pace.***

※

WHAT IF . . .

THEY LAUGH AT ME WHEN I AM EX-PRESSING WHAT IS IMPORTANT TO ME?

Then I will be in the position of taking up my own cause in a way that I want to present it. Then I can decide how to present myself. I may feel like I want to get even. I may make getting even my goal.

—and—

I can challenge their response by ignoring it and continuing to take myself seriously. I can continue with my presentation and refuse to be controlled or influenced by their behavior. I can allow others' their reactions while holding steady with my own beliefs.

※

***It is up to me to take myself seriously
even when others around me don't.***

———— ❧ ————

WHAT IF . . .

MY INFORMATION IS WRONG?

Then I may be corrected or told to redo my work. I may feel embarrassed or put down.

—and—

I can rethink my information or its origins and tell myself that information is neither right nor wrong. I can adopt the belief that people are stuck to certain facts because of their personal experience. To each of us, our facts feel like truth. I can judge my own work.

❧

When I am told that I am wrong, then I decide if I believe it. I decide if the "facts" are related to each person's interpretation of them.

❀

WHAT IF . . .

I MET SOMEONE AND FELL IN LOVE?

Then I might be shocked that this could happen to me. I might feel suspicious about this at first and doubt that this could happen to me. I may have closed myself off to the possibility of love and intimacy.

—and—

I may have to choose if I will stay with these old beliefs or allow myself to open up to what comes with love. Old issues and wounds may surface. I may be faced with old unresolved problems. I may choose to heal in a matrix of love with a new partner. I may choose joy over what I have known in my life before.

❀

I can love at any age or any stage
in my life.

WHAT IF . . .

I CAN'T FIND A MATE?

Then I need to look at how much focus I put on this search. Am I searching too hard? Is this search the only focus in my life? I may decide to look at the kind of people I am attracting to me.

—and—

I can learn what I want in a partner and what I don't want. I can choose to balance my focus. I can allow myself to become really interested in my life and trust for the time when a partner may appear. I can allow myself to learn to be alone and enjoy my own company before imposing or sharing it with someone else. I have many choices.

❁

Becoming comfortable with myself helps me to share myself in a healthy way with a partner.

❀

WHAT IF . . .

I CLEARED THE WAY FOR
ME TO BE ME?

Then I would free myself of distractions and the responsibility I may have felt to help everyone else with their dreams. I can attach myself in a healthy way to my own goals and dreams.

—*and*—

I can work in a methodical way to realize my dreams and goals. I can choose to believe in myself and act in ways that support that belief step by step.

❀

If I clear the way for me to become my truest self, then I start a journey that will hold my fascination for the rest of my life.

WHAT IF . . .

NO ONE WILL SHARE THE LOAD?

Then I may feel lonely and ignored. I may feel that no one cares about my well-being because they did not offer help when I needed it.

—and—

I can let others know when I need help. I can offer them the chance to help me and return the favor. I can tell myself that all people will not refuse help. I can open to receiving help from others. I can help them by being specific in my request. If there is still no one to help, then I can take only what I can reasonably handle and release the rest of the load.

❈

I help myself and others by making specific requests when I need help. I take on only what is reasonable to expect from myself.

❋

WHAT IF . . .

OTHERS WANT ME TO FAIL?

Then I will feel the pressure of their desire. I may get hung up in their scrutiny of me and their hope that I will not reach my goal. I may fear all their tactics.

—and—

I have the chance to use this opportunity to focus on what is really important to me. I can use their cues to spur me on to my goal. I can make choices that insure my success. I can choose a focus that honors me and loses my fascination with their hopes.

❋

I attach myself to my goal and use my best attempts to reach it, even when others want me to fail.

NOVEMBER

i am hungry
for my power
not to control but to remember
who i am, who i came here to be
and what i am to do.

i am hungry
for faith in me
that moves me to action

i am hungry
to feed on my birthright

I can feed on faith in myself
one act after another

I face my fear, apply my faith
I walk one step and then another

attend to this day and leave
the next one to itself

Faith is MY POWER
one step at a time.

Faith is believing
acting, spending
It is all I need

to wrestle fear to
the ground

Faith is remembering
that it is my next step

❀

WHAT IF . . .

I GIVE UP THE FEAR THAT MY LOVED ONES WILL LEAVE ME?

Then I will have some time on my hands and some space to try to trust. I may feel it is very hard to trust, and I may have good reasons for this. If I let go of the fear, I may have to practice my faith in loved ones.

—and—

I may also have to find new ways of taking care of myself. Without my fear, I may have to address the lack of trust and work on this. I may have to stop my fear with the relationship for it to be solved. I may have to look at and work on the defect of trust that exists within me.

❀

By letting go of my fear I can see my chance to trust.

❀

WHAT IF . . .

I BECOME SERIOUSLY ILL?

Then I may panic or operate from a position of fear and start fretting. I may feel shock at first and then anger. I may ask "Why me?"

—and—

I need to honor my feelings first, and then I can look at "Why Me?" from a different angle. I can look at the possible meanings this illness has in my life. Why me? Why at this time? What can I do with this? I can ask others for help, and I can let them help me.

❀

Asking "Why me?" gets to the heart of the issue when I am ill. I can look at the options before me and still choose the most fitting one.

WHAT IF . . .

I HOLD HOW I FEEL INSIDE ME?

Then I may develop illnesses or a deep sense of bitterness. I may try to protect others from the feelings I have inside, but in doing so, I create more difficulties for myself.

—and—

I can have long-term side effects from the times I choose to ignore or dishonor my own feelings. I have a choice each time I feel something—to ignore and act like it is not there or to honor it and bring it out into the open. Bringing it out in the open clears my body and it also clears how I relate to others.

❀

Taking care of my own feelings as they come up clears my body of unhealthy energy. When I do this I relate to others in an honest way.

WHAT IF . . .

I GET AUDITED?

Then I may become very frightened and panicky. I may begin to act like I have done something wrong. I may feel that I have made errors and that there is no way out of what I have done.

—and—

I will have the chance to look back over how I prepared my taxes and get professional accounting help if I decide it is needed. I also have the chance to see where I should have kept better records or appreciate the fact that I have kept good records. I may have to negotiate a change in my tax return. It can also be a moment when I see the hard work I have put in toward compliance. I can work through and appreciate the effort I made to comply.

❀

Whatever the outcome of my audit, I can find a way to meet my obligations.

❧

WHAT IF . . .

I HAVE A GOOD MARRIAGE
AND IT WORKS?

Then I may have to give up old ideas that told me marriage would be too hard. I may have to pay less attention to statistics that say most marriages don't work. I may change my focus from looking at others to looking at myself in relationship to my partner.

—and—

I may feel some loss or fear at taking the focus off others where I have a lesser degree of intimacy. Putting the focus on a deeper level of intimacy with my partner makes me look at my deepest needs. I can also see ways I need to grow.

❧

***Focusing on one major relationship
helps me understand myself and
another at a deeper level.***

WHAT IF . . .

I AM AFRAID TO GO TO THE DOCTOR?

Then I may refuse for a long time when I really could benefit by going. I may neglect my health and ignore some real needs that could be remedied. If I let myself go to the doctor, old issues and fears may come up.

—and—

I may have to rethink my priorities and face my own fear. I may have to decide if the fear is serving me more than the needed attention to my body. I can choose the one I will respond to— my body or my fear.

❀

The decisions I make about the fear I have affect my body today and in the long run.

❀

WHAT IF . . .

WORK TAKES TOO MUCH TIME FROM MY FAMILY?

Then I may face the fact that they do not know me or that we are drifting apart. Or they may feel that I am only there for their financial needs.

—and—

I have the chance to rethink how and when we are together. I can look at options for what we can do and how work can be arranged differently. Either way, it can be a time I use to reconnect with my family in ways that please us.

❀

When I find that my work takes me away from my family too much, I can rethink how I connect with them and make the necessary changes.

WHAT IF . . .

I CAN'T EVER HAVE MY OWN HOME?

Then I can think about what "home" means to me and I can let myself feel whatever I feel about it. I can think about the possibility of owning a home and ask myself how my thoughts affect my beliefs.

—*and*—

I can decide how important it is to own my own home and whether it's where I want to continue putting my energy. I can look at alternatives for home ownership that others have found despite their limitations. I can choose whether or not I will limit myself each time I think about this.

❁

I choose my definition of "home" and what I will do with it.

❋

WHAT IF . . .

I GAIN TOO MUCH WEIGHT?

Then I may be very dissatisfied with myself. I may also feel like eating more when I feel dissatisfied. I may feel like it no longer matters what I look like. I may give up listening and taking care of my own feelings. I may replace taking care of my feelings with eating.

—and—

I have the chance to determine what is really bothering me. I can see if there is discontent in my life and what's causing it. I can decide to be gentle with myself no matter what requests come from outside circumstances. I can choose a position of self-care and self-love each moment I think of food.

❋

I can choose self-care and self-love at each moment over other ways that I've attended to my needs before.

WHAT IF . . .

THE PERSON I TRUST MOST VIOLATES THAT TRUST?

Then I am likely to feel devastated. I may give up on others and this person for a while. I may feel anger and the need to strike back. I can let resentment stay in my body and fester.

—and—

I must honor my feelings and let them be. I can choose to work these feelings out of my system. I can also choose to let go of any expectation of this person in the future. I can decide whether I need this person in my life and I can choose how it will occur. I can define myself as I wish to be seen and present myself this way.

❁

When my trust is violated by someone close to me, I can decide right action for me based upon my current needs.

❊

WHAT IF . . .

PEOPLE TEAR DOWN MY WORK?

Then I may feel devastated if I am hooked on approval from others. I may feel embarrassed or silly. I may overlook what may actually be others' issues and take the blame on myself.

—and—

I can reverse this position. I can take the position that my work is good no matter what. I can trust my creative forces. I can look for reasons people tear down my work. I can allow for the possibility that they are acting out their own issues.

❊

***I choose to honor my work no matter
what others say.***

WHAT IF . . .
I HAVE TO FACE MY PARENTS BEFORE THEY DIE?

Then I may feel scared or powerless against the power I knew they had over me as a child. I can feel the power they had and the powerless sense I had as a child.

—and—

I can choose to reclaim my own power. If I decide that interaction with my parents is in my best interests, then I can approach them on an adult level. I can tell myself that they don't have to do or be anything different than who they are today. I can choose to be different. I can practice what I want to say ahead of time and listen to how I say it. I can present myself in a whole new way: one that reclaims my power as a healthy adult.

❦

I choose how I want to be with my parents as they age. I choose to present myself in a manner that pleases me.

❁

WHAT IF . . .

I USED FAITH THE SIZE
OF A MUSTARD SEED?

Then I might see that I can move the barriers that exist in my life. I might see that faith is power. I might see that faith is action. I might see that I have to choose action that honors me.

—and—

I could apply faith to help me understand all aspects of what I do and all situations that I face. I might find that miracles are more normal than I thought. I might also recognize that I must continue to act on faith once I see its strength.

❁

I choose actions that show my faith.

WHAT IF . . .

I HAVE TOO MANY PROBLEMS
ALL AT ONCE?

Then I may feel overwhelmed and withdrawn from others. I may feel unsafe and want others to take care of me. I may give up on my own ability to take care of myself. I may become bitter.

—and—

I have the chance to feel what I feel and then little by little organize a response to my problems. I can let go of the need to fix them all today. I can put them in an order that makes sense to me so that I can try my best to resolve them. I can ask for help and work with others to help myself.

❀

I can handle many problems if I
approach them in an orderly manner.

❀

WHAT IF . . .

I HAVE TO BE AWAY FROM MY PARTNER TOO LONG?

Then I may fear many things. I may fear that our relationship may be affected and that I will lose his/her love. I may feel lonely without a way to reach for my partner's comfort.

—*and*—

I have the chance to see our relationship from a new perspective. I can choose to appreciate what we have and what I miss. I can look for new ways to stay connected. I can also see what may need to be changed. I can rearrange priorities if I need to do so.

❀

I can see our relationship in a new perspective that helps me appreciate what is good and identifies needed changes.

331

NOVEMBER 16 ❧

WHAT IF . . .

I AM PRAISED FOR MY WORK?

Then I may be faced with how I handle compliments and good feelings about myself. I may find this very difficult to do.

—and—

I can look for the part within me that makes this difficult. I can decide if I want to keep this part. I can challenge the part that can't accept the good things it hears about me. I can look to the source of this belief and ask it to reconsider how it looks at me.

❧

I can look within for the part of me that cannot hear good things. I can honor where this part came from and invite it to see me in a new way.

WHAT IF . . .

I DON'T KNOW WHAT TO DO WHEN I AM ANGRY?

Then I can use this as a clue that I need to figure out what works for me. I can look at what I am doing now with anger and see if it is working. I can also see if I handle anger in a number of different ways. I can see if I need to change what I am doing now.

—and—

I can think about what is working for me when I am angry and see if it will work in most situations. I can also be sure that I know each time I am angry. I can ask myself if I believe it is natural to get angry. I can decide what is healthy for me to do with my anger.

❁

I choose to know about the place anger has in my life. I choose healthy ways to handle anger.

❀

WHAT IF . . .

OTHER PEOPLE DON'T KEEP THEIR PROMISES?

Then I am likely to feel let down and disappointed a lot. I may feel angry or bitter or I may choose to stuff these feelings and deny my disappointment.

—and—

I also have the chance to decide who I trust and how quickly I trust others. I can decide to let go of expecting others to keep their promises. I can choose to let others do as they will and relieve myself of hoping for a particular outcome with them. I can let go of resentment that comes with dashed expectations and false promises.

❀

I can let go of the expectations I have of others and the resentment that comes with unfulfilled promises.

WHAT IF . . .

I AM MISUNDERSTOOD?

Then I may feel like no one is listening. I may feel that what is so obvious to me should in fact be obvious to others. I may feel frustrated that my point of view cannot be understood.

—and—

I may forget how attached others are to their points of view. I may have to rethink how I can get them to listen. I may choose a different approach or let go of persuading.

❀

Being misunderstood offers me the chance to see that others have their views. Often I can approach them in a different way so they can hear my view.

WHAT IF . . .

THERE'S A GOOD CHANCE I WILL LOSE FACE IN FRONT OF OTHERS?

Then I may be frightened of this possibility. I may feel that I want to withdraw from this situation or that I don't know what to do.

—and—

I can choose to present myself in a way that leaves me feeling good about myself. I can let others have their views of me. I can choose the meaning I want for myself in any situation.

❀

I choose what I believe about myself in any situation. I give this more value than the views others have of me.

WHAT IF . . .

I FEAR LOSING THE HAPPINESS I'VE FOUND?

Then I may live in fear some or all of the time. I may feel I cannot trust what others say or what I feel because I will lose the happiness I've found anyway. I may feel that I cannot make any changes to eliminate my fear.

—and—

I can look at the origins of this fear. I can ask myself what event(s) in my past are still influencing me. I can recall and think about both the fears and the happiness in my past. I can accept that both happiness and sadness are natural parts of life. I can figure out what to do with both.

❈

I accept happiness and sadness as natural parts of my life. I choose to work through the fear of either one.

WHAT IF . . .

THEY DON'T UNDERSTAND THAT THEY HAVE TO PAY FOR MY SERVICES?

Then I am in the position of figuring out what my services are worth and making it known to those who need them. I may find it hard to stand behind my fees.

—and—

If this is the case, then I may have an issue of self-worth that I need to examine. I may have to look at the reasons I cannot charge a regular fee. I may have to look at how I let others' reactions affect what I do with my worth as it is expressed in my fees.

❧

I am willing to look at issues of self-worth as they come up in setting fees for my work.

❀

WHAT IF . . .

MY CHILDREN PICK BAD PARTNERS?

Then I may have to watch them learn lessons the hard way. I may have to see their pain or hear about it. I may find myself called on to rescue them.

—and—

I can look at their situations and see how I can support them without taking their lessons away or doing the lessons for them.

❀

I can deal with the pain of my children in a loving way without sacrificing myself to their situations.

WHAT IF . . .

I CAN'T FIND A JOB?

Then I may feel very frustrated and scared that I will not be able to support myself. I may adopt an attitude that is hopeless and find myself moping around for long stretches of free time.

—and—

I can choose better ways to spend these long stretches of free time. I can think of ways to prepare for work when it comes. I can present myself in ways that enhance my chances of getting work. I can also look for ways to earn income that I had not thought of before by considering and trying new things. I can put talents to work for me while I wait.

❀

I can discover how my talents, abilities and periods of waiting help me in my search for work.

❦

WHAT IF . . .

THERE IS NO NEED FOR THE WORK I DO?

Then I may feel a sense of uselessness. I may strive to convince others how useful I actually am. I may give up on myself and overdo my importance with others.

—and—

I now have the chance to look at how I want to be useful. I may choose to explore new ways and let go of the old ways. I may see reactions from others when I let go of the old ways and try something new. At any rate, I am the one who defines myself.

❦

I define myself and my usefulness in any situation. I have many choices in how I see myself and how I am useful.

WHAT IF . . .

I REALIZE THAT MY PARENTS VIOLATED ME?

Then I may feel shocked and totally disillusioned. I may feel confusion, sadness, anger, loneliness or a mass of other feelings that I cannot sort out. I may end up feeling like an orphan.

—and—

I can respect each of these feelings and allow myself all the time I need to work through each of them. I can honor all the questions, thoughts and opinions that come up as I face what I have found out. I can let go of any pressures I feel to respond in any certain way. I can make choices at each moment that take care of my deepest needs and honor who I am today.

❦

No matter what happened to me in my past, I am here today. I can choose to be present for myself and take care of all my needs.

❊

WHAT IF . . .

I HAVE A HARD TIME HAVING FUN?

Then I am likely to resist participating in what others call fun. I may not be able to recognize what is fun for me. I may not even know when I am having a good time. I may let others define what is fun for me.

—and—

I can choose to figure out what I consider fun. I can try things that look interesting to me and see if I enjoy them. I can wait for the time that it occurs to me that what I am experiencing could be fun. I will know it when I see it and feel the joy that comes from having fun.

❊

I can choose to find out what is fun for me and make it a regular part of my life.

❀

WHAT IF . . .

I AM NOT SURE WHAT TO DO?

Then I may feel pressured to come up with an answer right away. I may feel I have to know what to do. Not having an answer may feel very uncomfortable to me.

—and—

I can look at who is pressuring me to know the answer right now. I can choose to take my time and see this period of "not knowing" as a mere step to finding the the answer at the right time. I can allow myself to wait for an answer.

❀

I can let "not knowing" be okay and let it be a step to finding the right answer.

❀

WHAT IF . . .

THERE IS NO REASON TO LIVE?

Then I am likely to want to give up. I am likely to withdraw from others and see my life as worthless. I may know that I am depressed and not care about changing or I may want to end my life.

—and—

I may also see that having no reason to live is a way of saying I need to rethink what is around me. I need to look again for meaning in my situation or consider changing the meaning I have given to my present circumstances. I can ask for and receive help to see another way of looking at my life. I can choose to draw on the strength of others for a period of time.

❀

If I see that I have no reason to live, I can look for new meaning in my circumstances.

WHAT IF . . .

I GIVE UP THE FEAR THAT MY LOVED ONE DOESN'T REALLY LOVE ME?

Then I may give up old ideas about why people choose to be with me. I may have to see what others love about me and change the ideas I have about myself.

—and—

Then I may have to open up to receive love as it is given and take steps to return it. I may have to examine how I love. Do I love conditionally? Do I show love only after it has been shown to me? Could I be wrong about my opinion of myself? Am I more lovable than I thought?

❁

In giving up the fear that I am not really loved, I face coming up with a new way to see myself.

DECEMBER

i am hungry
for my power
not to control, but to remember
who i am, who i came here to be
and what i am to do.

i am hungry
for faith in me
that moves me to action

i am hungry
to feed on my birthright

I can feed on faith in myself
one act after another

I face my fear, apply my faith
I walk one step and then another

attend to this day and leave
the next one to itself

Faith is MY POWER
one step at a time.

Faith is believing
acting, spending
It is all I need

to wrestle FEAR to the ground

Faith is remembering
that it is my next step

Faith is MY POWER
made of faith
I am MY POWER
do my faith

I live MY POWER.

WHAT IF . . .

I FORGAVE MY FAMILY?

Then I would give up any bitterness and resentment I may have held for years. I would give up waiting for them to be different. I might feel a tremendous weight of sadness.

—and—

I might realize that I can and must do my own caretaking now. I cannot wait for others to do what I can now do for myself. I will feel a new freedom from expectation and disappointment. I am free to live as I choose.

❁

Forgiving my family if and when I am ready, frees me to care for myself.

❀

WHAT IF . . .

I TREATED MYSELF THE WAY I TREAT OTHERS I LOVE?

Then I might realize how I wish to be treated. If I put others first and think too much about their needs, then I may be neglecting my own needs. Do I deny them or forget them?

—and—

I may have to answer this question: "Who will take care of me if I don't?" I can ask who will see my needs if I don't. I can learn a balance between meeting the needs of others and taking care of my own.

❀

Each moment I have the chance to learn the right balance of caring for myself and others.

❋

WHAT IF . . .

I LOSE MY WAY?

Then I may be confused about how to proceed. I may look to others to lead me and put too much responsibility in their hands. I may expect far more from others than they are capable of giving.

—and—

I would feel the disappointment of putting others in charge of finding my way and then watching them fail. Then I could struggle finding the proper direction for myself. I could use my faith and try solutions that may occur to me.

❋

I can let my confusion be the first step to finding my way.

❃

WHAT IF . . .

I THINK THAT MY LIFE IS OVER?

Then I may feel very desperate and look to others to make me feel better or give me assurance. I may think I have contributed little to those around me.

—and—

I can choose to examine why I feel this way. I can ask for help from others, including professionals if I see the need. I can choose to see what is making me feel this way.

❃

When I feel that my life is over, I can look into this feeling to learn what to do next.

WHAT IF . . .

I BELIEVE ANOTHER PERSON HAS POWER OVER ME AND MY SITUATION?

Then I may feel helpless. I may feel the need to do things to keep this person happy. I may lose any focus I have on what is right for me and what I should be doing to take care of me.

—and—

I can look at the reasons I have let this person have so much influence over me. I can look at my past and see how it may be related to the power I have given this person. I can decide if I want to continue seeing this person in this light. I can ask myself if the power I think they have is real or if I am mistaken. I can release any image I have of this person and replace it with an image that doesn't hurt me. I can choose to see myself as a person of influence as well.

❈

I can choose who has influence over me and how much influence they can have.

❀

WHAT IF . . .

I LOSE MY SELF-RESPECT?

Then I may experience a deep depression. I may feel an overwhelming sense of worthlessness. I may let myself think that others see the same image of me as I do.

—and—

I can look at what led to these feelings and what I have done in the past to keep any self-respect. I can allow myself my feelings and decide on my next step. When I honor how I feel, then I have the chance to move forward.

❀

I honor how I feel at any moment.
I then move on to figure out
my next step.

❊

WHAT IF . . .

I LOSE MY HOUSE?

Then I may know the feelings others have had about being homeless. I may experience the discomfort of finding another place to live. I may feel like giving up. I may feel that nothing is secure anymore.

—and—

This may be a new experience for me. I have the chance to start over and set new expectations for myself. I can choose to tell myself to keep going. I can pull strength from within and from others who are willing to help. I can let my faith tell me that I am not alone. I may find a new sense of safety in the way others pull together to offer help.

❊

I choose to support myself with my thoughts and actions. I accept help from others. I learn and grow no matter what the situation is.

❄

WHAT IF . . .

THERE IS NO TIME LEFT FOR WHAT I NEED?

Then I may be asked to look at this question, "What do I really need?" I may feel neglected or overlooked. I may blame others for what I feel I didn't get.

—and—

I can look at my role in this situation. I can ask myself if I have allowed enough time to meet my needs. I can contemplate whether I left myself out or if I allowed others to overlook my needs. I can decide if I need to meet my needs now and ignore the time frame. I can choose to respect what I need and offer it to myself, regardless of time.

❄

I choose to be in charge of my own needs at any time.

❀

WHAT IF . . .

MY FRIENDS ARE DISPLEASED WITH ME ALL AT THE SAME TIME?

Then I may feel alone and lonely. I may feel that I am the victim of unfair treatment and that they owe me an explanation.

—and—

I can also quit waiting for them to change. I can decide that only I can change my part of the situation. I can look at my own behavior to see if I need to change how I interact with them. I can decide how I wish to present myself to them and others in the future.

❀

I can examine and change my behavior.
I can let go of my need for
others to change.

❀

WHAT IF . . .

OTHERS EXPECT ME TO CHANGE, BUT EXPECT NO CHANGE IN THEMSELVES?

Then I can look at their request for me to change. I may feel pressured to do things that do not fit with who I am. I may be faced with having to confront others who are not willing to listen to my side.

—and—

I can still choose to state my side and support it whether they listen or not. I can let go of the wish that they will change and hear what is important to me. I can state what is important to me, so that at least I can hear it. I can also choose to hear their sides. I can let go of my expectations for them to agree or even hear me.

❀

I state my opinion and make sure my actions support my words. I let go of the need to change them.

WHAT IF . . .

I LOSE FAITH IN MY RELIGION?

Then I may feel very lost for a time. I may feel that I have lost my sense of direction. I may feel very let down and even abandoned.

—and—

This is the time to look inside myself for any faith I may still have in something. I can allow this small amount of faith to help me know what is still worth believing. I can gather faith that makes sense to me and that fits me. I can also try to live my life without any personal faith in order to learn the role of faith in my life. Whatever I decide, I can choose to honor my decision.

❀

Whatever my response to personal faith, I can honor it and use it to make sense of my life.

✤

WHAT IF . . .

THE HOLIDAY RUSH
MAKES ME CRAZY?

Then I may feel overwhelmed and forced to behave a certain way. I may feel pressured by others to carry on a tradition that I find troubling for many reasons.

—and—

I can choose to stop being pushed by any kind of rush—holiday or other—and breathe deeply for a moment. I can decide what the holiday period needs to be for me. I have many choices. I can select what I need at this time.

✤

I can choose to make the holiday period what I want it to be. I release myself from all unwanted pressures.

WHAT IF . . .

I LOSE A LOVED ONE AT THIS TIME OF YEAR?

Then I may feel the worst sadness of my life. I may see others smiling and working themselves into a state of joy and even pressuring me to do the same.

—and—

I can let myself feel my feelings for as long as I need to feel them. I can let myself focus on what needs to be done between me and my loved one. I can let the influence my loved one had on me teach me even now. I can decide on my next step by paying attention to what happened in our relationship and what feels right to do now.

❊

I can let others have their own feelings, while I free myself from all demands and tend to my own feelings.

❀

WHAT IF . . .

SOMEONE STEALS MY IDEA?

Then I will feel violated. I may want to take revenge or legal action. I may want to threaten the person. Or I may imagine that I want harm to come to the person.

—and—

I can allow myself to have all of these feelings. I learn what my own ideas really mean to me. Now I can figure out what I need to do to protect my ideas in the future. I am likely to learn something new about my own boundaries.

❀

***When I recognize that I have been
violated, then I can set new
boundaries and protect myself.***

❦

WHAT IF . . .

I HAVE TO WORK TWO JOBS?

Then I may feel extremely tired and have little time for loved ones and activities that are important to me. I may feel stressed most of the time and stretched between several places.

—and—

I can look at my priorities now and rearrange them if needed. I can set reasonable short-term and long-term goals. I can look at all my options and ways to reduce stress at the same time. I can ask for help from others when I need it.

❦

I can choose to work hard, rearrange
what I need to do and receive
help from others.

❋

WHAT IF . . .

I RUN OUT OF MONEY AT
THIS TIME OF YEAR?

Then I may feel sad or bitter that I cannot afford whatever I think I should be able to buy. I may resent what I see others doing. I may also place a higher value on money than I do at other times of the year.

—and—

I can look at what money means to me. I can decide if it is the only way I can look at it or if there is another way to view it. I can think about giving and how I want to give. I can find alternate ways to give that do not involve money.

❋

***Running out of money can show me
what is of value to me.***

WHAT IF . . .

I CAN'T MEET MY FAMILY'S EXPECTATIONS?

Then I may feel a sense of shame, disappointment in myself and even embarrassment. I may have a sense that I am useless to my family.

—and—

I can decide what is reasonable to expect from myself. I can acknowledge how others feel and refuse to be trapped by those feelings. I can fulfill what I consider to be reasonable expectations of me and let the rest go. If my family is disappointed in me, and I refuse to be controlled by their feelings, then they get the chance to deal with what they can expect from me.

❀

I set reasonable expectations for myself and let others deal with their own reactions.

❀

WHAT IF . . .

I LET OTHERS' WISHES DICTATE MY BEHAVIOR?

Then at this time of year I may feel used and exploited. I may feel pressured to do and say things that do not fit with my inner wishes. I may ignore my basic needs.

—and—

I have the chance to clear the air and others' expectations. I can take each situation one at a time and state my own wishes. I can let others state their wishes first and then follow with: "Would you like to know what I would like in this situation?" I can wait for their response and follow it with what I would like to see. I can let them have their reactions to what I say, and I can refuse to fix any part but my own.

❀

I can hear others' wishes and state my own.

❀

WHAT IF . . .

I OVERSPEND?

Then I may feel depressed or disappointed in my own behavior. I may also feel a little high from my purchases. I may refuse to look ahead for the consequences of my spending, preferring to deny the costs to me.

—and—

I can look at what is behind the purchases. Was I trying to present a certain image? Was I trying to soothe an inner wound of my own? Was I trying to buy my way into a situation that I could not easily enter? I can study my own behavior and learn from it.

❀

I choose to observe my spending habits, especially at this time of the year, to determine what these habits reveal about me.

❀

WHAT IF . . .

I CAN'T FIND THE "RIGHT" GIFT?

Then I may feel rushed, frustrated and pressured to do something according to someone else's idea of what is "right." I may feel I have to present a certain image that fits in with others' expectations of me.

—and—

I can choose what is reasonable to expect from myself. I can choose my own expectations as guides for my behavior. I can present the image that I feel comfortable with. I can refuse to be instructed by the "shoulds" of the holiday season. I can let others learn how I see myself. I can let them react in any way they choose.

❀

I am free to present myself in the way that suits me. I let others react the way they will.

WHAT IF . . .

I FEAR OTHERS' DISAPPROVAL OR DISPLEASURE WITH ME?

Then I may want to withdraw from them. I may fear that no matter what I do I will not "get it right" and I may give up. I may end up feeling that there is something wrong with me.

—and—

I can determine how I will feel about myself in any situation. I can choose behaviors that fit me. I can let others have their expectations from me without changing what I do. I can also see if anything needs changing in my behavior.

❀

I can let others have their reactions to me. I can choose behaviors that fit who I am. I can make changes if I need to do so.

❋

WHAT IF . . .

I FEEL VERY SAD AT THIS TIME OF YEAR?

Then I may get panicky or full of pity. I may even feel despondent or want to end my life.

—and—

I have the chance to face these feelings to see what's at the bottom. I can choose to express this sadness when I feel it. I can ask for help from those I trust or seek the help of a counselor. I can choose to know what these feelings mean and how I can grow from them.

❋

My sadness at this time of year has a meaning that can help me to learn and grow.

WHAT IF . . .

I HAD TO START OVER AGAIN?

Then I may feel a very strong sense of hope-lessness. I may be overcome with the sense that I do not want to try. I may convince myself that it is useless to try.

—and—

I can choose to support these awful feelings. I can remind myself that others have probably felt the same way when and if they had to start over again. When I am ready I can start with one step at a time. I can ask myself, "What do I need to do now?" I can look at how I can meet this need. I can use any faith I have to search for the right steps to take. I can let others help me.

❧

If I have to start over again, I can guide myself one step at a time, and find new ways that please me.

❋

WHAT IF . . .

I AM ALONE?

Then I may feel really sad, bitter and depressed. I may also find that I ache to be with my loved ones. I may long for happier times from my past.

—and—

I may feel this more strongly now than at any other time of the year. I can choose to face my fear of being alone. I can take this time to connect with my own loneliness and do something about it. I can get help from any personal faith I have and from things or persons in my surroundings.

❋

***I have choices to make when I fear
being alone that can help me cope
with any loneliness I feel.***

❈

WHAT IF . . .

I REALIZE MY RESPONSIBILITY TO MYSELF AND MY ROLE WITH OTHERS?

Then I can let go of pretenses, or any false image I have set up for myself with them. I can still let others be themselves.

—and—

I can be with them in an honest way. I can learn what is reasonable for me to do with or for others and what I must do alone. I will feel a sense of purpose and do what I can, when I can. I will take care of my own needs when they come up. I will feel a responsibility to find the right action for me in any situation that I face.

❈

Knowing my responsibility to myself and my role with others leads me to my purpose.

❀

WHAT IF . . .

I FIND MYSELF DEPRESSED DURING THE HOLIDAYS?

Then I will find that I am not alone with these feelings. I may feel there is a real reason to be depressed. I may want to withdraw or strike out at myself and others.

—and—

I can look at the sources of my feelings. I can examine my expectations of me and others. I can rethink expectations and choose different behaviors that may move me through the depression I feel. I can let myself feel sad as long as I need to feel sad. Then I can think this through and open myself to other feelings and to help if I need it.

❀

I can be a friend to these feelings, find their source and move through them.

373

WHAT IF . . .

I FIND NO PEACE AT THIS TIME?

Then I can think about my expectations of the season. I can allow myself whatever I feel and assess the circumstances and beliefs that have led me to this unsettled feeling.

—and—

I can look at the circumstances and beliefs and accept reasonable expectations from myself. I can refuse to instruct myself to feel any way other than how I'm feeling. I may come to know a deep peace from honoring what I feel inside.

❁

I can assess my circumstances and beliefs and the feelings that come from them. I can find peace by respecting my own feelings.

❀

WHAT IF . . .

OTHERS OFFER MORE TO THEIR LOVED ONES THAN I DO?

Then by comparing myself to them, I may continue to feel a sense of disappointment in myself. I may long to do more. I may long to be someone else.

—and—

If I choose to compare myself, I can lose touch with the gifts that I do bring to loved ones. I can lose touch with what is unique about me and what I bring to our relationships. I can regain that understanding by finding reasonable expectations for me and offering what I can to those I love. I can honor myself by remembering what I give to others.

❀

I remember my own uniqueness.

WHAT IF . . .

I HAVE NO FAMILY OR RELATIVES?

Then I may feel very alone, depressed, sad or just the longing to be in the company of loving people. I may wish to be someone else that I think has it better than me.

—and—

I have the chance while I am alone to connect to myself and my own unique person in a new way. I have the chance to enter into my loneliness and treat it tenderly. I can refuse to make any rash decisions or demands on myself. I offer love in the best way I know how to love myself. I am a good friend to the terrible loneliness that I feel.

❀

With no one else around, I still have a precious connection to make—with myself. I treat myself with tenderness and love at this time.

❁

WHAT IF . . .

I COME TO BELIEVE THAT THERE IS A CONNECTION BETWEEN ME AND EVERYTHING ELSE ON THE PLANET?

Then I will give up hopeless feelings and ideas that I am useless. I will give up the idea that I have nothing to contribute.

—and—

I will look for and know the unique role I have in the web of life on this planet. I will understand that others have their unique roles and that we are all gifted. I will honor and take care of the gifts I have. I will decide how I want to use them. I will honor gifts in others.

❁

If I believe I have a connection to everything on the planet, then I will play my part and share my gifts.

WHAT IF . . .

I REALIZE THAT I HAVE EVERYTHING
I NEED RIGHT NOW?

Then I have to let go of excuses that keep me
from what I am to do in my life. I will leave fear
behind.

—and—

I will see the work that is right for me to do. I will
recognize the path that is right for me to take. I will
interact with others in a way that is respectful to
them. I will have no need to control others. I will
see and respect our differences and similarities. I
will contribute to my environment in a unique way
and recognize that others do the same.

❀

I have what I need and know that each
step I take is right action. I can trust
what I know to be right for me.